Simple Gardening in Pictures

Rob Herwig

Simple Gardening in Pictures

Or how to have a beautiful garden and free weekends as well

WARD LOCK LIMITED · LONDON

First published in Great Britain in 1973
by Ward Lock Limited, 116 Baker Street,
London, W1M 2BB
© Elsevier Nederland N.V., Amsterdam-Brussels
1971
ISBN 0 7063 1068 3

Text filmset in 9pt Times New Roman

Made and printed in Great Britain by
Cox & Wyman Ltd, London, Fakenham and Reading

Contents

Preface

There are dozens of 'complete' gardening books on the market. They all claim to tell you everything you need to know in order to turn your garden into a veritable paradise. It is quite true, they do tell you this, the trouble is finding the one piece of information you want at any particular moment, in the midst of all the information that you may never even refer to.

The object of this book too, is to turn your garden into a paradise, but the approach is very different and much more practical. Gardening has its problems, and sooner or later all gardeners run across the same problems. This has become very apparent to the author who in his normal daily journalism has received letter after letter and phone call after phone call all dealing with the same few problems again and again.

What this book does is to take these problems and show you ways of solving them that are not only practical and permanent but which also make attractive features of your garden. Thus you not only solve the problems but you also finish up with a far more attractive garden than when you started.

Gardening should also be fun, and if this book makes gardening more fun for you, more rewarding and less of a chore, then all the hard work that has been put into it will have been amply rewarded.

Forcing-frame

The forcing-frame is very useful for sowing garden plants early in the season. In this way, for comparatively little money one obtains the newest and most select summer flowers much earlier than when one has to rely on nursery-grown plants for the flowerbed.

In the old days frames were generally made of wood or concrete, with a glass pane to admit the light. In strong sunlight this had to be screened or the young plants would be scorched. Nowadays there are very reliable, double-walled plastic frames. The advantage is that anyone can erect them in a jiffy.

On this page you can see several stages in the construction process. With the aid of a spirit-level the whole thing is set upright, but one side slopes about 10 cm, so that rainwater cannot settle on the roof. Care must be taken over securing the corners.

If the frame can be warmed a little, this means sowing can begin as early as February. Very little power is needed to keep this double-walled, well-insulated frame free from frost. The photographs show you how it works. The soil-warming cables can be connected to the mains at 240 V and use little current. For this box, a 60 watt cable is sufficient to raise the temperature of the seedbed by about 10 °C. In order to gain maximum benefit from the warmth, a sheet of polystyrene foam is first laid on the soil. This not only provides a good foundation for the cable, but also insulates the frame from the cold ground. Leave a narrow opening along the edge and lay a little extra sand under the middle of the sheet, thus assuring good drainage. The easiest method of securing the cable is with strips of plastic adhesive tape. Lay the coils at least 10 cm from one another. Then place 3–5 cm of clean builder's-sand over the cable, to hold it in place. This sand is necessary for the even distribution of the warmth. Over the sand lay a piece of plastic wire-gauze, and on top of that 5 cm layer of seed compost. Spread it evenly and moisten thoroughly.

The photograph *right* shows an electronic feeler, consisting of two electrodes moulded in plastic. With the aid of an electronic switch (obtainable as a construction-kit) the fairly technically minded amateur can make himself a drought-alarm, which gives an audible signal when the compost needs watering.

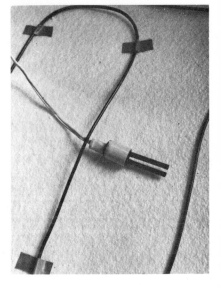

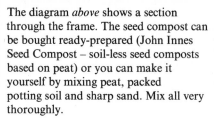

Above left putting in the seed compost. *Above centre* shows the surface neatly divided by thin bamboo canes into small compartments. Different sorts of seeds can be sown in each compartment. These can be sown straight from the packet (*above right*). Take care the seeds do not fall too close together; 1–2 cm apart is about right.

Sowing is even easier with the new pelleted seeds, which are pressed in the soil one by one (*below left*). They germinate particularly well. After sowing the soil is covered with a thin layer of pure white sand (*below right*).

The diagram *above* shows a section through the frame. The seed compost can be bought ready-prepared (John Innes Seed Compost – soil-less seed composts based on peat) or you can make it yourself by mixing peat, packed potting soil and sharp sand. Mix all very thoroughly.

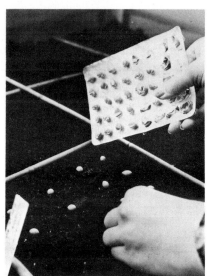

Covering with sharp sand is much better than sprinkling with sieved compost, because the coarse structure of the sand allows air to pass through. Firm down the sown portion with a board or the flat of the hand to promote contact between the seeds, the soil underneath, and the covering layer (*above left*). Then give a thorough watering, so that the compost is soaked without, however, washing the seeds from their place (*above centre*). Finally, close the box and switch on the heat (*above right*).

After about 4 days just check that the soil is still damp enough and give any water needed. As long as there is nothing showing above ground there is no need for screening, and, for that matter, this frame of matt plastic never lets too much light through.

When the seedlings have successfully emerged, the box can be opened a little during the day, but in this case evaporation will be much greater and so water must be given every day. Seedlings grown under glass must be shaded from damage by strong sunlight.

Seedlings can be successfully grown on the windowsill, too. Use a window-case with a clear lid. By sowing directly into little pots (3 seeds to a pot) you can save yourself pricking out. For plants of the poppy family and other seedlings that transplant badly, this is a good system to use in the frame, too.

After a time, unpotted seeds sown in the warm or cold frame will need to be pricked out (set wider apart). This can be done when the seedlings have developed two true leaves (first come two seed-leaves, but these don't count). Put your hand under the roots of the little plants and lift up the soil. Try to loosen the plants without damaging the roots. Don't leave the seedlings lying about: plant them again straight away. The most convenient way is to prick them out into peat pots. For planting-out use ordinary potting compost, preferably mixed with 20% sharp sand, otherwise the nutrition might be too richly concentrated. If your seedlings are somewhat thin, then you can safely plant them out rather deeper. Press down the soil evenly and put the pots back into the frame. If you embed the pots a little in the remaining seed-compost, this will reduce the chance of the soil in the pot drying out (*small photo right*).

The result of these sowing and
transplanting activities can be seen here.
In the foreground are a few slow
germinators (*Impatiens*), still not
advanced enough for pricking out; all
the rest are in pots, mainly peat pots.
The pricked-out plants have been
sprayed now and then with liquid
manure, which has furthered their
growth a great deal.

Night-frosts are usually over and done
with by the end of May. Then the young
plants, whose roots will by then be
growing through the peat-wall of the pot,
can be planted out in the open ground.
Here they will find conditions rather
hard at first because the protection of
the frame is missing. To give them a
good start it helps if the soil where they
are to be planted is improved with peat
and a little granular fertilizer. Water
regularly at first if the weather is dry.

Below right is an example of *thinning out*.
This is necessary if you have sown too
thickly. If the seedlings touch each other,
then they are too close.

Manuring

In their natural state plants don't need manuring, they make their own manure. Every leaf, needle and twig that falls, rots away on the ground into a thick layer of compost, which will provide fresh nutriment. Further nourishment is of animal origin and the rest comes from the soil itself. If the soil is poor, then only plants which can make do on comparatively little nourishment will grow there, whereas on rich ground a completely different assortment grows. Garden plants have been gathered together from almost every country on earth. They are natives of the most diverse soils and among them have widely different food requirements. The fact that in practice they thrive nevertheless is only due to the fantastic adaptive powers most plants possess. But we can considerably improve the growth and well-being of most plants by giving each one the position which most resembles its natural situation.

Because in the garden as a rule no layer of natural refuse covers the soil to supply the roots with nourishment, we have to add manure. In its simplest form this is done by spreading compost (see page 136) or well-rotted cow or pig manure over the soil. Usually this layer is then dug in shallowly, but this is not essential. It is always best to disturb the soil as little as possible.

There are countless fertilizers, both organic and artificial. Among the organic manures are compost (sometimes artificially enriched), stable manure, dried stable manure, enriched peat products, ground animal refuse, etc. The best-known artificial manure is the common granular fertilizer, but along with this are countless pills, liquids, and mixtures. Because in practice it is difficult to determine whether one fertilizer is better than another, each manufacturer says that *his* product is absolutely the best. But often the world-shaking invention stops short at the wrapper, and the contents turn out to be good old-fashioned granular fertilizer, possibly with some extremely dubious additive.

For the average garden, that from the start has been properly manured and improved (see page 132) a mulch of rough stable manure or compost each year between the shrubs and in the borders is all that is needed. Home-made compost is, of course, also very good. Apply at the rate of half a cubic metre per 100 square metres. Use up to a maximum of 3 cubic metres per 100 square metres on exceptionally poor dune-soil or land. If you wish you can omit the stable manure every other year and replace it by artificial fertilizer in granular form. Use 2–4 kg per 100 square metres. Stable manure and compost are best put on in the autumn (when they also serve as a protection against frost), artificial fertilizer in the spring, because its nutritious content washes away more quickly (washed out of the soil by rain or irrigation).

With the *lawn* things are rather different. A lawn is a highly unnatural affair, since the grass is repeatedly cut very short. Hence vigorous growth is required, which the grasses can only manage if a good deal of nourishment is given. The nutritious matter in the soil is very quickly exhausted, because the roots of short-mown grass are also very short. Long grass also has long roots (see diagram). In a layer of some 5–15 cm, the whole food-cycle is played out. Artificial fertilizer is best able to supply

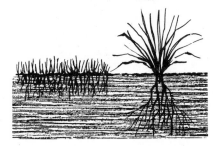

the extreme nutritional requirements of the lawn. It is easy to apply, particularly if soluble or even liquid manure is used. A lawn that is cut every 4 or 5 days in summer can use 1 kg granular fertilizer per 100 square metres, plus an equal quantity of special lawn-fertilizer. Now

15

and again try a different artificial fertilizer to find out which suits your lawn best, because in every garden the nutritional requirement varies. The only certain way to find out which fertilizers your garden lacks is to make a soil-test, or have one made (see page 129).

The technique of manuring is as follows. Rough manure or stable manure can be ordered from farms or manure-dealers or can be bought in dried form in plastic bags. The manure is lifted on a fork and shared out among the plants. Don't lay any big clods against stems or on top of plants. Granular fertilizer is scattered by hand. For the lawn a fertilizer-spreader is preferable, two types of which are shown on this page. The risk of scorching (yellow patches, caused by too much fertilizer on one spot) is greatly reduced, because spreaders of this sort distribute the grains evenly. Always clean metal spreaders thoroughly after use, for artificial fertilizer promotes rust formation.

For grass, there are also slow-acting fertilizers. The secret of these is that the nutritional salts are gradually released as the temperature rises. By applying in April, the normal 10–12 kg per square 100 m can be distributed all at once, and will be sufficient to last until August.

Various ways of spreading the artificial fertilizer granules can be seen in the photos.

Below left by hand. This is the most tiring method; definitely not recommended!

Centre with the aid of a special spreading bucket. The grains fall through an opening in the bottom.

Above right with a wheel-mounted spreader – the best method.

The plant is a chemical factory, the leaf the reaction chamber. The sun's heat causes evaporation, resulting in the movement of sap causing the roots to take in moisture. In that moisture are found foodstuffs in completely dissolved form. They can only pass through the membrane of the root cells if the concentration of food-salts *in* the plant is greater than that outside it. If we supply too much manure, then the stream flows in the opposite direction, the plant 'becomes empty', and then we have what is termed scorching.

When the food supplies have reached the leaf, then there, with the aid of chlorophyll or leaf-green and under the action of sunlight, sugars are formed. For this process carbon dioxide is also needed, which is absorbed from the air. During this process oxygen is given off. The sugars are carried to all parts of the plant, where they build up plant cells.

Because granules cause scorching when they fall too close together, various devices have been invented to distribute them evenly, at least on the lawn (see page 16). It is at least as simple, however, to apply fertilizer in liquid or soluble form, and this method virtually eliminates scorching. The large illustration shows you an attractive gadget for attaching to the end of a hose. The reservoir is part-filled with liquid manure (*below left*) and then topped up with water. Then the knob is turned and the fertilizing fluid comes out automatically in the dilution of 1:60 or 1:30 (according to choice) in the spray of water.

There are various sorts of liquid manure among which a foliar feed with growth-hormones and trace elements working through the leaves of the plants are probably the best. For garden use I recommend the big (10 litre) pack. Soluble manure is supplied in powder form and can also be sprayed very well by means of this 'Garden Gun'.

Below right we show another aid, the 'Siphon-aid' from the United States, a simple little appliance that sucks up

liquid manure from a bucket into the water-jet. It works, however, only with very simple sprinklers, also with hand-sprayers, which give little counter-pressure, but not with most oscillating-sprinklers.

Tiles and stones

Tiles, natural stones, terrace-slabs and other stone paving occupy an important place in most gardens. Not always the loveliest place, alas. When used imaginatively they can create stunning effects. In the 'twenties and 'thirties someone came up with the idea of using slabs of natural stone as paving for paths and terraces. 'Flagstones', preferably of irregular shape, were then the epitome of garden 'chic'. They are still in use, but only in older style gardens. They have been largely replaced by the 'washed' concrete slab, a usually unreinforced slab with a top layer of gravel. An indiscriminate use of these is not to be advised, however, for there are many other materials on the market. In the choice of the material price will obviously play an important part. Grey pavingstones, 30 × 30 cm, are the cheapest. Most builders lay them in an unimaginative strip at the back of your new house which they then dignify by calling a 'terrace'. It is, however, worth the trouble of spending a bit extra here, for such a piece of pavement has little aesthetic appeal. Washed concrete slabs are also inexpensive, but are not particularly attractive. The quality of aggregate used in making such slabs varies greatly. Pretty and not too expensive are coloured slabs, which can be grey, black, or pink. Distinctive slabs are those in which large flat pebbles lie among the finer gravel. Then there is also brownish and even green aggregate: in short, a wide enough choice. You have only to take care you get good quality. Another thing that's worth a test: walking barefoot on the paving you choose. Broken gravel hurts your feet, black copper-slag slabs are also very

sharp. Walking is fairly comfortable on round gravel.
Blocks of natural stone are about 2 to 3 times as expensive as washed concrete slabs or smooth concrete terrace slabs. Irregular flagstones have rather fallen from fashion, but a terrace of rectangular slabs of natural stone is always very pleasing. To avoid subsidence or cracking they are best laid on a bed of concrete. This also means that thinner stone can be used.
An attractive effect can also be achieved by laying bricks in a similar fashion, preferably also on a concrete bed. There are various patterns available. There are also concrete blocks 10 × 10 × 10 or 6 × 6 × 6 cm, which have a blueish colour.
Perhaps the most attractive of all is a terrace of natural cobblestones. They can often be obtained from demolition merchants or local councils. The most attractive are red granite, but grey granite flecked with quartz or limestone cobbles are also effective. Small cobbles are the prettiest, laid in sand on a well-drained gravel foundation, particularly in the well-known curved pattern. This is the paving used in the sitting-area on page 66.

page 66.

Key to the picture on page 20.
1 Øland stone. 2 Granite in gravel flag. 3 Alp-green with black quartz in gravel flag. 4 Basaltine in gravel flag. 5 Selected loose stones. 6 Coarse brown pebbles in yellow pit-gravel flag. 7 Meuse-pearl in gravel flag. 8 Carrara marble with nacre in gravel flag. 9 Black concrete blocks 6 × 6 × 6 cm. 10 Yellow limestone. 11 Green porphyry cobble, irregular shape. 12 Kotah stone (India). 13 Black concrete slab with scoured surface. 14 Coarse white mixed with brown gravel. 15 Black diabase. 16 Red granite. 17 Mid-grey granite. 18 Green porphyry, regular shape. 19 Norwegian sell. 20 Yellow pit-gravel with black broken stone in gravel flag. 21 White granite. 22 Yellow-ochre granite. 23 White Dolomite. 24 Pink-grey porphyry. 25 Black slate.

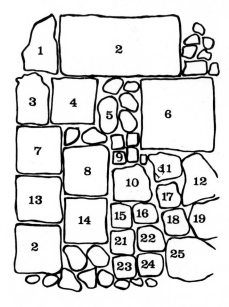

Paving plays an important role in the layout of the modern garden. In the photo *above* you see how washed concrete flags form a distinct pattern, into which are set panels of simple bricks. This is much more attractive than the gravel flags alone.

The photo *right* gives a striking example of the use of paving to divide the lawn from the border. This avoids the tedious business of clipping the edges, and it also does away with that strip of bare soil at the part of the border that collects so many weeds: you can plant right up to the paving. Besides, there is always a dry path on which one can walk in winter without damaging the grass.

If terrace flags or bricks are laid properly you will not have any difficulties with subsidence later on. By doing the job properly in the first place you save yourself the annoyance of having to re-lay the paving. If the foundation is no good the stones will keep on working loose and sinking. The drawing shows the correct way of laying flags, which above all must be laid on a firm foundation. Rubble 10–20 cm in depth forms a drainage-layer. Over this is placed a thin layer of sand, so that the flags can be laid flat and level.

Large expanses of paving must be given a slight slope, so that rainwater can drain off, but you mustn't overdo this slope. For well-laid flags, a drop of 1% (i.e. 1 cm per metre) is sufficient. *Below* is another photo of paving with small cobblestones or pebbles. It is quite difficult to do this well, so one would do better to leave the work to a professional. For the finished result, see page 66.

After laying, the small stones are hammered home, and lastly fine silver sand is swept between the crevices (*right*). While it is usually thought that a spirit-level can only be used for achieving a level pavement, this is not in fact so. Many spirit-levels can be adjusted to give a reading which will automatically give you the correct fall.

With the advent of washed concrete slabs and the disappearance of the traditional rock gardens, large round pebblestones have come to play an important role in gardens. They harmonize exceptionally well with gravel flags, and their interesting form gives the garden an extra dimension. Moreover – and this is of practical importance – they are particularly useful for filling up all kinds of little corners left after laying the flags. Against the housewall they ensure that drips from the eaves run smoothly away, especially if there is a layer of rubble underneath.

Raised beds can be created in which the stones can be laid between the plants. This not only looks better than bare earth or stone chippings, it is also more practical and requires less maintenance.

It is even possible to cover a garden completely with really coarse stone chippings and a few large stones, among which one can place troughs of plants (*far right*). Maintenance is extremely simple.

Smooth pebbles can be bought from builder's yards or garden contractors. If the stones are in a shaded place they may need treating with an algicide.

Cobblestones, large or small, must always be laid on a bed of rubble or gravel, so that water can easily drain off. Eventually the stones become dirty, through leaves collecting in the gaps. These must be constantly removed (*centre*) and after several years the cobbles need to be taken up and cleaned. A hired concrete-mixer is excellent for this cleaning job.

The patio designed for a sculptor (*right*) is covered in fired floor-tiles, laid on a concrete bed. The same tiles are used for the interior. This is an excellent way of linking outside and inside. Frost-resistant tiles must of course be used. *Below* is a small front garden, which looks wider than it really is because of the red bands of red facing stone laid between the paving slabs. Washed slabs with a variety of surfaces have been deliberately used, in order to show the effect. Most people would probably prefer a somewhat quieter effect.

Under certain circumstances a pleasing effect can be created by laying slabs or tiles obliquely to the direction of the path. The example *left* shows how this idea can be applied in practice. The grass edge is easy to mow. At the most it will need trimming once a month.
Below is an example of imitation travertine, known by the name of Strukturit. These concrete slabs are absolutely frost-resistant. The material is in combination with blue concrete blocks.

Various examples of paving.
Right small concrete stones, which hold together on account of their special shape, so that no edging is necessary.

Left an example of washed concrete tiles with bricks on edge used for decoration between them.
Far left below a beautiful circular pattern made of selected stones laid in a bed of mortar. Expensive, but a worthwhile feature in any garden.
Below centre Bands of large pebbles (in cement) between washed slabs. A very

pleasing way of solving the problem of what to do when the slabs are too small to fill the space provided. Moreover, it enlivens the surface appearance. For choice, washed slabs should not be laid directly next to one another.
Below right a highly professional pattern made entirely of ordinary facing stone, split into small pieces. See also page 39.

Ground-cover plants

There is a growing demand for ground-covering plants, both in private gardens and in public parks. Plants of this sort are just what the modern garden needs. Few people really have enough time to keep everything in the garden spick-and-span. Wherever there is bare soil, weeds will keep springing up, and it takes a lot of time to pull them *all* up. Ground-cover plants simply smother the weeds. By means of their dense, creeping growth, with offshoots constantly taking root, they form quite quickly a green or flowering carpet which covers the ground entirely. The patch is green and stays green, and needs scarcely any maintenance. Leaves and other organic debris that collects between the plants is best left there. It forms a good natural mulch. If there are no fallen leaves, scatter a little fertilizer between the plants now and then. Here is a short-list of easily obtainable ground-cover plants:

Cotoneaster dammeri. For sunshine or light shade like a humus-rich soil.
Hedera helix. The common ivy, and its variegated-leaved varieties make excellent ground-cover. Prefer some shade and soil rich in humus. Alongside trees and walls the ivy will, of course, climb as well as covering the ground.
Juniperus horizontalis. Prefers full sun in a sandy or peaty soil, and a position where it will not suffer drought.
Pachysandra terminalis. (photographed on this page): tolerates a good deal of shade and is excellent under trees.
Saxifraga umbrosa. This makes a very fine ground-cover for positions in light or quite dense shade.
Sedum spurium. Another permanent plant, this time for sunnier spots. Flowers profusely and beautifully in the summer. For chalky soil or clay.
Vinca Minor. The periwinkle grows untidily perhaps, but it covers the ground well and tolerates shade. Prefers humus soil.
All the plants listed here are fully hardy.

Page 28: various sorts of Sedum and *Euphorbia myrsinites* creep among the stones.
Above left: Cotoneaster dammeri, perfect for not too shady places.
Above right: Cerastium biebersteinii.
Above: Juniperus horizontalis 'Glauca'.
Below right: Perfect ground-covering in the rock garden.

Hedges

You can choose between a low small hedge, which need be no more than an optical division, and a high hedge, which gives real privacy. The growing of a thick, 2 metre high hedge takes time. *Privet*, the fastest, takes 7–10 years about it. Often people plant tall, therefore costly, conifer hedges, but in many cases these large specimens never thicken out into a dense hedge. Smaller plants and more patience are a better way to a fine hedge. Among broad-leaved shrubs these are particularly good; *privet* (loses some of its leaves in winter and is a greedy feeder); *hornbeam*, leafless in winter; *beech*, will not tolerate too much wind, holds its dry leaves in winter; *hawthorn* makes a fairly thick hedge; *holly* makes a good dense hedge but needs shelter from winds in northern districts.
Of the conifers, *Taxus baccata* is the best for hedges. It tolerates shade, quite a lot of wind, grows slowly, but is very

dense. *Thuya* has a fresher green colour, but cannot tolerate much wind. Some varieties of *Chamaecyparis*, e.g. the dark green '*Alumnii*' and the blueish '*Triomph van Boskoop*', are suitable for high hedges in fairly wind-sheltered places, but they become quite thick eventually. The method of planting a hedge can be seen on these pages. First a trench is dug (*below left*) into the bottom of which is dug some organic manure.
The deeper and wider this trench is made, the more successfully will the hedge grow. If the plants are dry when they arrive, stand them in water while you are busy digging. This is particularly important with conifers. When the ground has been well prepared, lay the hedging plants in a row so that you have the right number at the required distance.

the other fills in the earth. Afterwards the ground is firmly stamped down. A stretched line will ensure a neat row. After planting an abundant watering must be given in the stamped-down gully which should lie a little lower than the surrounding land. Then the water will run to the roots. Directly after planting the bushes should be cut back

by about 1/3, in order to force them to branch out at the bottom (*above right*). *Below* a good example of a hedge that affords privacy. In this case *Carpinus betulus*, the hornbeam, was used. You can get much the same result with *Fagus sylvatica*, the beech, with the difference that the latter also offers protection in winter since the dead leaves all stay on.

Any good catalogue will state how many plants you need per running metre.
It is best to have two people doing the planting itself (*above left*). One holds the shrubs at the desired distance and depth,

Hedges generally do not show up to best advantage in photographs; nevertheless, here are a few examples.

Above: Carpinus betulus, hornbeam.

Above right: Two tints of *Ligustrum ovalifolium*, privet.

Centre a light tint in *Chamaecyparis*, and *Centre-right* a blue-green *Chamaecyparis*.

Below left: Thuja occidentalis.

Below right: Taxus baccata.

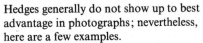

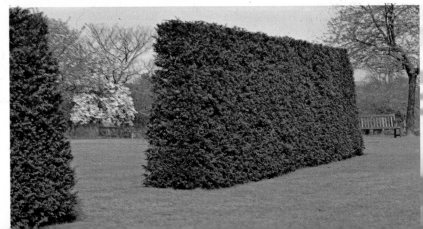

Most hedges need cutting or trimming twice a year: at the beginning of June and in mid-August. Conifer hedges need cutting only once a year.
Ordinary garden shears, preferably with wavy-edged blades are normally used for cutting hedges (*above left*). For larger hedges, it pays to purchase an electric trimmer. Be sure to buy a good one (*above centre*). There are various other tools available for cutting hedges, such as the hand-clippers (*above right*). Young conifer hedges are best cut with secateurs, because it is generally sufficient

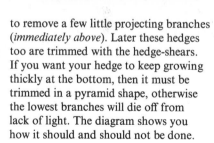

to remove a few little projecting branches (*immediately above*). Later these hedges too are trimmed with the hedge-shears. If you want your hedge to keep growing thickly at the bottom, then it must be trimmed in a pyramid shape, otherwise the lowest branches will die off from lack of light. The diagram shows you how it should and should not be done.

Pruning

The pruning of shrubs and trees is really a very simple process, but almost every gardening amateur is scared stiff of it. Furthermore, the need for pruning is often vastly overrated.

In principle every shrub or tree grows best unpruned. After all, no shrub or tree gets pruned in the wild. Cases do occur, however, where pruning is necessary and useful: at planting, in order to correct bad growth, for special effects (e.g. hedges, shaped trees) and when a shrub is growing too big or too

thick. Also, to encourage fresh growth, which in some plants requires very drastic pruning (see list in *next* column).

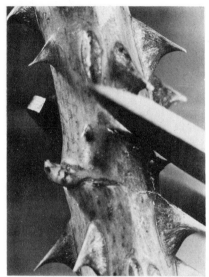

Roses are a special case: see page 38. The detailed photographs on this page show you what pruning really consists of: a cut directly above a bud or a thinner twig. The position of this bud indicates in which direction the shoot will grow out; thus the bud you choose determines the later shape of the shrub. Pruning is done when planting in order to help the plant put all its effort into establishing a robust rooting system as rapidly as possible. Prune only torn or damaged roots. In the case of trees, any branch growing inwards across the crown had better be removed, otherwise it might start scraping against another branch.
If a bush is bare at the bottom, then new growth can be encouraged by sawing away some of the lowest branches

directly above young shoots.
In practice one must differentiate between shrubs which flower on the current year's wood and shrubs that flower on older wood. Shrubs of the former kind are also late in flowering, from July on. Often in the spring a great deal of wood is taken out, in order to keep the bush compact. This encourages flowering.
Shrubs that flower on the previous season's wood cannot be pruned in the spring, since this would remove the wood on which the flowers would be produced. If necessary, these plants should be pruned directly after flowering. Below are a few groups of shrubs which require special treatment: 1 In the spring remove all the frost-caught wood thoroughly, if needs be level with the ground.
Amorpha, Buddleia, Caryopteris, Ceanothus, Cephalanthus, Escallonia, Hedysarum, Hypericum, Indigofera, Lespedeza, Perovskia, Rosa, Spiraea × bumalda and *Spiraea japonica.*
2 In the spring or after blooming prune hard. All branches older than 2 or 3 years must be taken out.
Berberis (leaf-shedding varieties), *Cornus alba* and *C. stolonifera, Exochorda, Forsythia, Holodiscus, Itea, Potentilla, Rubus, Sorbaria* and *Weigelia.*
3 Directly after flowering remove all wood that has flowered, up to the young side-shoots.
Deutzia, Philadelphus, Prunus triloba (at 3–5 nodes of the stem, *Ribes, Syringa* (if the bush must be kept low).
4 Only if the plants are becoming bare at the bottom, now and then cut back a portion thoroughly, immediately after flowering.
Artemisia, Calluna, Erica, Lavandula.

Above stainless pruner. The blades are interchangeable and are coated with Teflon. With the knob you can adjust to three positions: close, half-open, completely open.
Below mini-pruner for light work. For general garden use this is too light, but as a second or third pruner it comes in useful.

Above pruning-shear on the anvil-principle, the sharp blade (*above*) presses on the soft, flat anvil (below). Lever-operation and internal spring. Teflon-coated.
Below The old-fashioned pruning-knife is only usable in practised hands. It is handy nevertheless as a general garden knife.

Above Secateurs of traditional form, very reliable in their simple construction. Blades generally of steel, not interchangeable. External spring. Handgrips covered in plastic.
Below Small pocket pruning-saw, foldable, for light sawing.

Extreme left a fine model pruning-saw, indispensable when you have a few sturdy trees in your garden. With this saw branches 15 cm thick can be removed safely and easily.
Left another pruning-saw with a pistol hand-grip and special teeth.

For the middle-sized garden a serious, solidly built pruner is of prime necessity. Choose from the three models at the *top*, price from £2 to £3.
If you have trees, then you also need a light pruning-saw, such as is shown *below left*. For thick rose-bushes and other reasonably heavy pruning-work, the lopper (*above left* on the following page) is an extremely useful aid.

Below a large pruning bow-saw. With this one can not only cut thick branches, but also saw timber into small logs. Particularly useful in the larger garden, where it would be used quite frequently. Whatever you prune, take care to make a straight, clean cut, leaving no jagged, split or flattened branches. These show that the pruning-shear was blunt, or too

At the top a lopping shear or lopper, a long-handled pruning-shear. Excellent on thorny bushes or if one doesn't want too much bending.
Above a long-arm pruning-shear for out-of-reach high branches. You can make the handle and the draw-string as long as you want.

At the top one of the heaviest models of pruning-shears with wrought-iron parrot-beak-blades and long wooden arms. With this one can easily cut through a young tree. In general a light saw is handier and cheaper.
Above A further detail of the pruner at the end of a stick, as is shown in action on the left.

small for the job. Any split can become a home for parasites, which later attack the wood. When you prune Malus and Prunus, the danger of wound-infection is particularly great. With these species it is best to paint the pruning-wound with a pruning compound.
In trees of these families, and also in fruit-trees, a canker sometimes appears, an ugly disease of the branches with rough wounds and brown, cracked patches. Such cankered portions must be cut right back to the sound wood. For this one uses a pruning-knife (photo on page 36) or a special, curved canker-knife. After the operation the wounds should be treated with a disinfectant and sealed with pruning compound.

Left you see a rose bush immediately after the winter. There is even a few hips left on, but much of the wood has been hit by the frost.

Above is the same bush after treatment. It has been pruned short; on each little branch are 3–5 'eyes'.

Rambling roses, especially if you manure them well, make long, thin shoots in the summer that appear out of the older wood. Take care not to break them; tie them securely, for these are the main-branches on which next year's flowering-wood will appear. Above such a young shoot you can at the beginning of August (after flowering, therefore) cut out the old, thick branch altogether, preferably with a lopper (see page 37). If you do this in 3 or 4 places, this will thin out the bush tremendously. Remove all the old and worn-out wood, too. This yearly revitalizing is the best care for your ramblers. Be sure to do it at the beginning of August: if you prune in the spring you'll rob yourself of many blooms.

Left and right the pruning of a weeping rose: a rambler, which has been refined on the stem. Clearly we must distinguish between long, outwards-growing shoots, which must be kept as they are, and the younger twigs growing crosswise upon them. In the small illustration you see how these are all pruned back to 3 points.

A rose bush flowers on new wood, therefore it can be cut back vigorously in the spring. If in March one leaves not more than 10 cm of branches standing, then one will get low rose bushes. If one prefers taller bushes, then leave up to 30 cm above ground. This will enable the plant to weep attractively.

Left you see how a small shrub, flowering on wood of one year's growth (in this case *Spiraea × bumalda* 'Anthony Waterer') is cut back in the spring. All but 5 cm of the wood is removed. The new pink sprouts are already forming, and in August will ensure a compact but richly blooming little bush.

Garden path

The garden path as we used to know it, covered with gravel, no longer appears in the modern garden. Only over very large expanses, where any other surfacing would be too expensive, are such paths still used. In most smaller gardens there are nearly always two obligatory paths; one leading to the front-door, the other to the garage. The picture *alongside* shows an exciting way of making a path leading to a front door. The path is laid in a mosaic of cut facing-stones in two colours. This is only one of many possible ways of making a path like this a little less conventional. On the following page you can see further examples of paths that are out of the ordinary.

The garage-path to this house consists of two tracks of flagstones with grass in between. For several reasons this is not an ideal solution: there are too many edges to trim, the grass in places becomes worn in patches and pot-holes

come into existence too easily. It is better to cover the path entirely with an attractive surfacing. It is precisely in the small garden that the path has a useful function, namely to spare the grass. Lawns will suffer only a limited amount of treading: if there is too much there will be bare patches. In a well-planned garden there will be paths in these well-trodden places, so that the grass remains grass and your garden has a better appearance. Analyse the customary walks and make the route practical, and give the path also an optical function as far as possible in the layout of your garden. This is what has been done in our 'demonstration garden' that you'll constantly be coming across in this book.

39

Very often a path is laid in the garden without any preparation, or at most a thin layer of earth is put down. Through treading and through frost-action subsidences will eventually occur, giving the garden a neglected appearance. It is therefore better to lay a path well from the start. As foundation well-rammed rubble is used, preferably in two layers as in the photograph *alongside* coarse rubble (1) and fine-crushed stone (2). Above this, a thin layer of sand (3), which should preferably be well watered-in. The remaining loose sand is sufficient for the tiles or stones (4) to lie level. Finally the surfacing can be mechanically pounded, but this is not necessary if the foundation was well-rammed.

The small photograph *above* shows a path impregnated end-grained wood blocks.
Centre a charming example of a path in natural stone in bow-pattern.
Right an unusual stair-like path of round concrete stepping stones.

Raising tuberous plants

If you want the dahlias, gladioli, begonias or other tuberous plants in your garden to start flowering early, it is necessary to start them indoors. This can begin as early as March, though generally the tubers are set out at the beginning of April. If you have a greenhouse, of course you will use this for the tubers, too (the first weeks under the table). You can also start them just as well in a warm or cold frame, or in the house on a windowsill. The bulbs or

tubers must not be too warm, 20 °C is quite warm enough. The handiest method is to plant the bulbs or tubers straight into peat pots, using ordinary potting compost. You can see this in the photographs. Did you know that in begonia tubers (*above left*) the *hollow* side is the top? Keep the soil fairly moist and after a few weeks the young shoots will start appearing, and shortly afterwards the first little roots will push through the pot wall. Only when the last night-frosts are over (generally about mid-May) can you set the young plants, which will already be growing vigorously, in the garden. Put some good soil round the peat pot, then the roots will grow out quicker.

Labels

As you can see in the *adjoining* photograph, there are many ways of providing plants with a label. Regrettably there are no permanent labels. Through the influence of wind and weather, but above all through sunshine, any ink, no matter what its composition, will fade after a few years. Moreover, the white or yellow plastic of the label itself will also become weathered.

In practice I like best a simple labelling machine (*below left*) which can be bought for about £1. The strips are later stuck on white, stand-up boards. In the general picture you can see a label of this kind in the *rear centre*. At best, they last 5 years.

If you want a quickly written, reasonably readable label, then use a special felt-tip marker such as is shown farthest back in the large photo. However, it will not last more than 2 years. The result depends on your handwriting. All

plastic labels are suitable.

A new invention is the black label (*below centre*) on which you scratch the name with a sharp stylus so that the underlying white layer becomes visible. It works just like a scraper-board. There is a lot of work, too, in making labels by means of Letraset. The result, however, is extremely professional (*above right* in the large photo). But even these fade with the years.

In botanical gardens engraved plastic or sometimes metal labels are used, but for this you need a costly engraving machine.

Mulching

Mulching is the practice of covering the ground with a layer of organic material, leaf-mould, peat, compost or manure. To understand the point of doing this it is worth seeing what happens in the wild. In natural surroundings all the foliage, twigs and other refuse falls down among the plants, so that the ground eventually becomes wholly covered with a thick layer of humus. This not only protects the ground from rapid drying-out, and prevents the soil from becoming compacted by rainfall, but also gives the plants extra nourishment. In private

gardens it is often otherwise. All the leaves are neatly raked away and the plants stand in the bare earth. In the long run this is bad for the soil and for the plants. By mulching one is really restoring a natural condition. One can use weed-free compost, hedge-clippings, straw, peat, leaf-mould, and farm or stable manure. The mulch should be put on fairly thickly, about 5 cm, otherwise weeds will grow through it. In the *uppermost* photographs you see how first the ground is thoroughly weeded between the plants. Afterwards a thick layer of peat plus other fertilizing material is put down. One great advantage of mulching is that it vastly reduces weeding.

Dividing

Many permanent plants and also some low and bushy shrubs can easily be increased by dividing or splitting them. Both operations come to much the same thing and are carried out in the spring (March–April), or late summer (August–September). In the photographs you see how easily this can be done. *Above left* the clump is lifted out of the ground with the aid of a spade or fork. Next one pulls the clump apart with the hands. If this doesn't succeed, then you will have to use the spade to chop the clump up. Each root portion must have at least one growing bud. The clumps can be divided into two or three pieces, or into dozens, each piece consisting only of one little sprig (the small photo *below*; the plant is *Vinca minor*). This should only be done when one requires a large number of new plants quickly.

Generally one retains larger portions, as in the case of the *Helenium* hybrid in the photo *left*.

When permanent plants have been growing for some time they often outgrow their space. They should then be lifted and divided, and the best pieces kept. The soil should be dug anew, manured, and the pieces re-planted. The diagram shows how to divide Dahlia tubers.

In gardening man is interfering with nature. He does this to try to make plants grow better than they do in the wild. Often, however, he does the wrong things and his garden becomes a cheerless demonstration of tidiness and misunderstanding of nature. The well-known Bearded Irises, which flower magnificently in May and June afford an excellent example of good and bad cultivation. These irises make thick fleshy root-stems which stick half-out of the ground. Out of these, the vigorous roots grow straight downwards. The rhizomes (the thick, fleshy creeping roots) grow outwards all the time, leaving behind in the middle of the plant the half-dead root-stems which do not flower. After four or five years you have plants with an ugly mass of dead rhizomes in the centre. That is the moment to rejuvenate your irises by dividing them.

In the photo *above left* you see such a plant at the beginning of April, with all the good shoots on the outside of the clump. *Above right* the plant has been dug up. Division can begin. *Immediately below* the knife points to the oldest,

cracked rhizomes which have finished their useful life and can be discarded. Carefully the plant is split into pieces, and you see the result *below centre*. At the top are the old root-stems, which still have roots but have formed no shoots. Below these are a few larger pieces with young shoots capable of flowering. At the bottom are five very

young rhizomes which show just how small you can divide the plants.
Below right re-planting. Another good time for dividing irises is the beginning of August. Costly varieties can be quickly increased by dividing them at least once a year into as many small portions as possible, though the smaller the portions the longer they will take to flower.

Low fencing

Nowadays there are various construction-kits on the market, with the aid of which one can fairly speedily make a sturdy low fence. *Above left* you see how it comes out of the box: all in pieces. The planks don't appear in the photo. They must first be treated with a black impregnating material such as creosote. You can of course also paint them, but after a few years the wood looks very grubby. If you use an impregnating material you have only to brush over lightly every few years to make your fence look good as new. The steel parts are covered in plastic and so are rustproof. In the example shown was a little gate, which had to be assembled completely before being set in the ground. All you need to assemble a kit like this is a suitable screwdriver. The gate is positioned exactly level, then, while one person holds it, the other can firmly stamp down the ground.

The actual fence consists of wooden panels screwed to metal beams of a fixed length. These are assembled before erection. *Adjoining* this column you see such a panel, in which the planks have been neatly screwed into place side by side. The first or last part will not always fit exactly, as is the case in our example. On page 47 you can clearly see how to the right of the gate there was room for only two planks before the wall was reached. With a metal saw it is simple to make the beams the right length: a touch of paint on the saw-cut stops the iron from rusting (photo page 47, *below left*). When a section of the fence is ready, it is screwed on to the gate-post (*above right*). You will need to stretch a line so that your fence will be straight. The next post is now attached and dug in. You can still

see the sunken foundation-plate, which gives the necessary stability. In soft ground this is not always sufficient; since the gate has to put up with quite a lot of movement. All that need be done to make the post really secure in such a situation is to pour dry, ready-mixed concrete into the hole, moisten and allow it to set.

48

Above left the same gate as shown on page 47.
Above right a post-box to match.
Immediately above a taller version of the gate.
Right centre a light and playful-looking little fence of painted metal.
Below right the contrasting white of the gate makes it clear where the entrance is.

High partitions

The more we are confronted in our daily life with noise and people, and the more we are crowded in by neighbours, the more we feel the need for privacy in the garden. Hence the growing interest in higher screens. With their aid one can create one's own patio. The photo on the *left* gives a good idea of just how effectively one can keep one's neighbours out of sight.

Partitions where people can just look over the top fulfil no function. Therefore

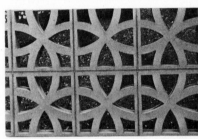

the minimum useful height is 1.80 m. If your privacy problem is not one of noise only of sight, then you can choose one of the many open partitions of which you see examples on the following pages. There are concrete elements in countless forms. They require a solid foundation and can be fixed with the aid of special glue or with mortar (page 51, *below left*).

A modern wood-wall, a more decorative version of what used to be called a fence, is easy to make yourself. The material generally used is deal, impregnated with creosote or a modern wood preservative. The slatted jalousies were homemade (page 50, *below left*). You can also see them on page 66. The panels are attached with screws to hardwood piles. The advantage of screws like these is that they have no 'ugly side'. The method of driving in the piles is shown on this page. With the aid of a drainage-spade (photo on page 135) or an auger an improbably narrow but deep hole is dug. For a 2 m high wall the pile must go at least 70 cm into the ground. The narrower the hole, the more solidly the ground will hold the pile. With a spirit-level and measuring-stick everything can be easily and correctly positioned. The illustration shows the setting of a concrete pile (weight 80 kg).

Attaching the panels is now a relatively simple matter. The diagram *adjoining* shows three effective ways of building up the wooden parts (which for example could be 17 cm wide by $2\frac{1}{2}$ cm thick). *Above* with the panels set at 45°. From one angle only there is an unimpeded view; looked at squarely the view is completely blocked.

Centre the planks are set horizontally, alternately on both sides of the standing pile. Here again the wood-wall has no ugly side, and thus is very suitable as a partition between neighbours. It can of course be also arranged vertically, as shown in the *lowest* diagram. Finally a good tip for those with a small purse. Fix in the piles (wood or concrete), and attach as a temporary measure only cheap reed-mat (*above right*). This will last for 3 to 4 years. Later on perhaps the wood-wall can be used to replace it when there is enough time or money.

51

The large photograph on the page
opposite gives a good idea of how the
privacy problem in the small garden can
be elegantly solved. The pierced wall
blocks are of German manufacture
(H. Meyer, Rheydt). Part of the wall is
covered with *Aristolochia macrophylla*.
The picture *above* is a good example of a
wooden dividing-wall. The heavy,
wooden uprights are attached alternately
on either side of a light metal frame.
Maintenance is minimal because the
wood has been treated with a wood-
preserving impregnating material.
Right a wall of irregular concrete pillars.
It needs absolutely no upkeep. It would
look even better with a few plants
growing over it.

The latest screen wall blocks of Bredero
Concrete was designed quite a long time
ago by the famous architect Rietveld.
The L-shaped 'Lorenzo blocks' can be
mortared or glued in various positions
and provide an unusually striking
design. A completely different impression
is given by the airy dividing-wall shown
below. The elegant screens are mounted
in a steel frame.

Planting perennials

The planting of hardy herbaceous perennials presents few problems if it is done in the spring. Autumn planting, however, can easily result in frost damage. Order the plants as early as possible to make sure of getting the best of the stock. When planting-time comes round, your order will arrive in a small case or box (*below left*).

Open the box at once, water any plants that have dried out and, unless you can plant them the same day, store them in litter in a frost-free shed or garage. It is best to choose a cloudy day for the planting and very important not to plant in waterlogged or frozen soil. The plants are packed variety by variety and each is labelled. First lay the plants out where they are to grow, but don't plant them yet. Only when the arrangement is just to your taste (*below centre*) should the plants be put in one by one (*below right*).

Borders
of annuals

A good seed-border begins on paper.
Start in the winter by picking out a
number of plants that go well together
as regards colour, height and flowering
season. You will find all the information
you need in any good catalogue or a
book about annuals.

At the appropriate time the seeds should
be sown in the warm and/or cold frame.
Many can be grown from seed sown *in
situ* in the open ground – but bear in
mind the tip on page 59, then the result
will be much better. On the adjoining
page you can see an example of an
annual border, specially designed for
you. You don't have to sow all the
plants yourself, some varieties can be
bought as bedding-plants.

The photos on this page show borders
of bedding plants; *far right* is the
climbing plant *Ipomoea*.

An example of a border composed entirely of annuals sown from seed. Dimensions 4.20 × 1.50 m.

1 Lobularia 'Violet Queen'.
2 Chrysanthemum paludosum.
3 Dorotheanthus bellidiformis.
4 Nemophila insignis. 5 Lobularia maritima 'Sneeuwkleed'. 6 Tagetes patula 'Ruffled Red'. 7 Nemesia strumosa 'Compacta Tom Thumb'.
8 Phlox drummondii 'Nana Compacta'.
9 Iberis umbellata 'Pumila' (= 'Nana').
10 Nigella damascena 'Miss Jekyll'.
11 Scabiosa atropurpurea. 12 Delphinium ajacis 'Imperiale'.
Plus, for contrast,
13 Buxus sempervirens. 14 Sedum spathulifolium. 15 Onopordum arabicum. 16 Ajuga reptans 'Rubra'.

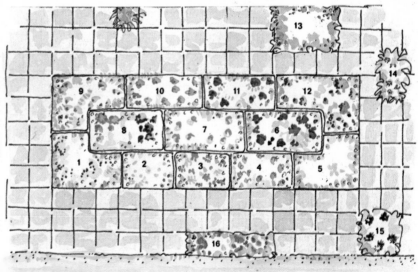

The garden centre is probably the best place to buy bedding-plants. As a rule the quality of the stock at garden centres is very good, but once in a while it happens that the clods are too small or dried out. *Below* you see the difference between a good plant (in the pot, *left*) and a poorly grown specimen of a similar plant. *Bottom* another pot-grown plant showing good root growth.

Before planting the stock out in your border improve the soil with a peat or a compost-based fertilizer (*below centre*). Afterwards set the plants close enough together for the whole surface to be closely covered once the plants grow away. 20×20 cm is usually a good distance (*below right*).

Sowing in the open

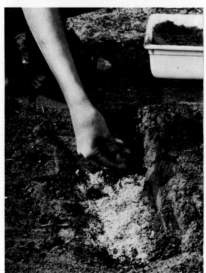

It may not look very impressive in the photographs, but this is one of the most useful tips in the book, especially if you like growing flowers from seed.

It concerns sowing seed in the open, in the place where later they are to bloom [a method that avoids the need for pricking-out (see page 13)]. The first and most obvious rule is not to sow the seeds too close together: if you do you will have to spend an awful lot of time thinning them out.

First of all, you must sow the seed *in rows*, that will make it easier to distinguish the seeds from the weeds when they both come up at the same time. They don't have to be precise rows, as long as there is a line of some sort. After the plants have been thinned and have grown up these little rows will no longer be visible.

Secondly, and even more important, where a row is to be made, push the garden soil a little to one side (*above left*) and fill it straight away with moistened potting-soil or compost. Press this well down (*above centre*). Then sow thinly (*above right*), sprinkle the seed with sand (*below left*) and finally give a good watering (*below right*).

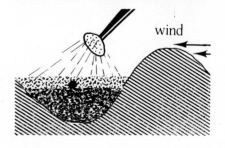

wind

Colour arrangement

It is the way you mix or marry colours that determines whether your planting is successful. One good combination, *below*, is the biennial Forget-me-not *Myositis sylvatica* with an *Azalea*. The detail *left* shows *Cosmos bipinnatus*.

Above left: Campanula pyramidalis, one of the loveliest blue garden flowers, mostly raised as a biennial. *Above right* a beautiful form of *Pelargonium* with the fairly unfamiliar blue *Felicia amelloides. Below left* the warm orange of *Antirrhinum majus. Below right: Myosotis sylvatica* in two tints.

Sunken gardens

In recent years more and more people have been creating sunken gardens. Why is this adjunct to the garden – always pretty expensive – coming so much to the fore?

The drawing *above right* on this page lets your clearly see the most important advantages. A sunken sitting area is of particular benefit in smaller gardens. By lowering the level you achieve a number of advantages simultaneously. First of all, you can't be seen so easily. This is important if the garden is right beside the street or if the neighbours are close by. Furthermore the noise of traffic is considerably reduced when one withdraws into the sunken area. Then there is less wind, so you can lounge outside and get a tan a couple of weeks earlier than your neighbour.

Yet apart from these benefits the sunken garden also adds a new dimension to the garden, creating changes of level which do much to relieve the monotony of any normal flat site.

The psychological aspect is also important: the feeling of pleasure and protection that most people experience when they take their ease in a sunken garden is well worth the effort.

The depth to which you sink the garden may vary from 20 to 80 cm, according to your needs. Good drainage is essential, especially on clay soil, so that a heavy rainstorm will not change it unexpectedly into a swimming pool. In general a simple drainage with sand and a few plastic drain-pipes is quite sufficient.

By the combination of a sunken garden and a 2 m high partition-wall (see page 50) pretty well every privacy problem can be solved.

From left to right:
Sleepers. Generally the cheapest solution. certainly for do-it-yourself men. No foundations are needed, and they are heavy enough and stable enough to be laid on soft ground. Cut them to the required length with a crosscut saw and join them with very long nails, previously drilling the holes, so that they are firmly fixed.

Units. There are numerous concrete units for sunken gardens, of which this 45 cm high, U-shaped model is one of the most attractive. A layer of rammed-down rubble is sufficient for the foundations. See also page 148 for further possibilities.

Wall. Almost every form can be built with bricks. This round wall (see also page 66) was entirely brick-built. Calcareous sandstone was used for the foundation. This is the most expensive solution, but sometimes it is the only possibility.

Top two pictures of a garden made with sleepers, the dimensions only amount to 5×10 m. By making differences in level, with the sunken lounge as the deepest point (40 cm), the garden appears larger than it really is.

Far left the beginning of the construction: the lowest layer of sleepers is arranged and laid in a little white sand. Surplus soil is removed and the plant-beds receive a good quality of garden soil. The second photo shows the same garden directly after planting.
The photo *above* shows a round sunken lounge with a barbecue.

The pleasant intimacy of the sunken lounge invites a variety of activities. *Right* an invitation to laze in the lounge made of sleepers, the construction of which is shown on the next page. Pelargonium, roses and heather bloom round about. In the background a trough with rockplants, and *Kochia* in a tub.

The sunken garden *below*, made of concrete blocks, presents a more active picture. In the background you can just see a second sunken recess, which serves as a sandpit. By inserting a piece of tough plastic one could make a cheap play-pool instead.

On this page you can see how the sunken garden in the *top* picture on page 64 was made. A pit of this kind can be easily built in almost every garden, with little trouble or expense. Firstly you excavate the soil, which is carried off in a wheelbarrow. In this case the size of the railway sleepers (2.60 m) determined the dimensions. One side of this sunken garden was built of little concrete blocks, which can be stacked in various manners. *Left* you see the construction of the foundation: a layer of calcareous sandstone. *Below* a photo of the paving. *Below left* the plan.

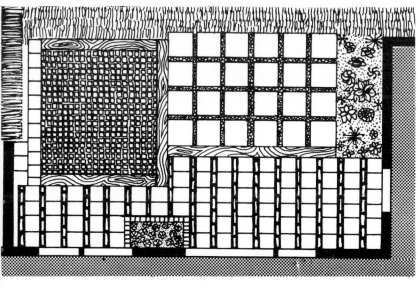

A typical problem-garden is shown in the *adjacent* photograph. On the other side of the wire-mesh fence there is a fairly busy thoroughfare. Because of the noise, the wind, and above all the lack of privacy, it is almost impossible to sit outside at the back of the house (*left*). In the *lower* photograph you can see how the privacy problem was solved. To gain privacy a 2 m high slatted wood-wall was made; such slatted structures actually break the force of the wind more efficiently than solid structures. The large round sunken garden is 80 cm deep and incorporates a matching round pool. The floor is covered with natural cobblestones. The lighter pattern is made of cobbles of a whiter colour.

The use of pesticides is in many cases superfluous

Garden plants are usually troubled by pests and diseases sooner or later. The problem for the gardener is to steer a middle course between using every pesticide and fungicide in sight to keep his plants completely free from any possible infection – in which case he will do more damage than good – and not using them when they really are needed – which could mean losing plants. Manufacturers of insecticides even advise you to spray when no insect is in evidence. 'Preventative spraying' is the fancy name, but all too often it is unnecessary, though of course it boosts manufacturer's sales.

It is worth looking at what actually causes plants to be attacked by blights and pests. There are four main causes:

1 *Exclusive cultivation of one crop* (monoculture). In nature different plants grow mixed up together. The bugs and blights that affect one plant are unlikely to affect their neighbours. Thus a balance is maintained. In the garden where, for example, you have a whole bed of roses or dahlias, any bug or blight that attacks one plant is likely to spread to the whole lot.

2 *Cultivated strains are more sensitive.* In the garden the great majority of the plants we grow are specially selected strains, varieties or crosses. These give us bigger, more beautiful flowers, but also often weaken plants, more prone to attack by bugs and blights.

3 *The plants are treated wrongly.* Together with point 4 this is the most frequent cause of a plant becoming sickly. If a plant needs sun plant it in sun, not shade and vice versa and don't plant plants that like clay on sandy soil, and don't put rockplants by the pond. In almost every garden this rule is sinned against, and sickly plants are the consequence.

4 *The plant suffers from deficiency.* Many plant diseases are deficiency diseases. Plants, like people, not only need food but need the right foods. We demand

67

formidable growth-performance (for example in the lawn), and for this the required nourishment must be provided, otherwise things go wrong.

Only by checking and rechecking the above four points can one successfully combat pests and diseases. If we fail to attend to one or more of these (especially items 3 and 4) then the plant will become weak. It is weak plants that fall prey to pests and diseases, seldom healthy ones. One unhealthy plant can provide a home for a bug or blight that will then move on and attack the healthy plants.

As proof, trials have been carried out in which the same rose has been grown in two groups: one was well-fertilized and placed in a sunny position, the other stood in the shade in poor soil. Before long the latter group had aphis. Then roses from the two groups were jumbled together (the roses were in plant-tubs). Not a single aphid went over to the healthy bushes. A few plants are difficult to keep altogether free from attack. Among the roses there are some which, though very lovely, have a notoriously weak constitution. '*Virgo*', a

magnificently formed white rose, for example nearly always has a certain amount of mildew. Another frequent culprit is the shrub *Euonymus* (Cardinal's Hat), which is very susceptible to attack by the cocoon-thread moth. There are several more of these problem plants. In such cases the gardener may consider it worth his while to take the necessary steps to protect his precious plant. If he does, he should make sure that he doesn't go for those pesticides and insecticides that do lasting damage to the soil, or – even worse – lasting damage to his own health. Unfortunately such products are the most easily obtainable. For centuries materials of vegetable origin have been known that destroy parasites. The best-known of these are derris powder and pyrethrum (a dust made from the flowerheads of a certain chrysanthemum). These products are as safe as any on the market. Moreover, they are on sale in aerosol packs, so that application is easy. There is even a pack which contains both pesticides. It is provided with a special valve, so that it can even be used upside down (*above right*).

Against fungus diseases such as mildew there is not a great deal that can be done. Sulphur is a fairly harmless medium that does some good. It can be obtained in liquid or powder form. A dispenser for applying the latter is seen *above left*.

Damage from wild life

n wooded or rural districts wild life can cause quite a lot of damage. It is principally a matter of nibbling by hares and rabbits; once in a while deer can also cause trouble. Dogs and cats, although not strictly 'wild' as a rule, can also be destructive to plants.

The best protection is always a complete fence of wire-netting, sunk about 20 cm in the ground and at least 1 m high, preferably inclined slightly outwards. The entrance to the plot can be closed with a wide-mesh steel grating of the cattle-grid type, across which few animals will venture.

There are various products on the market to keep off wild life damage, such as fluids with a repellent smell in which rags or rope are soaked and then wrapped round trees or bushes. There are others that one sprays on the bare wood in winter. Netting round the tree trunks is also effective and lasts longer. A little sporting-dog or a fierce tomcat will also be a very good defence for your garden against incursions of wild creatures. The dog can be trained to leave the flowerbeds alone. Fieldmice you can entice by offering food at certain places, for example by planting *Helianthus tuberosus*. The cat often lies in wait near such a plant. Moles can be got rid of by placing a smoke-cartridge in the passages. A very effective ruse is to stick a child's little plastic windmill in the grass: the vibrations seem to keep the mole away – except in calm weather, naturally.

Tools

Most garden tools and appliances are to be found on other pages of this book. The remaining gardening aids you will find together here. The garden vacuum-cleaner on the *opposite* page looks perhaps as if it's meant as a joke, but in the United States and in continental Europe it is a perfectly serious instrument that is used in many gardens for sucking up mown grass, leaves and other refuse. It can also be used for blowing: leaves are directed to one place and finally the heap is sucked up. Such a machine is certainly useful in larger gardens, especially in these days when help is hard to come by and few people have time to resort to sweeping up leaves with an old fashioned beesom.

A rather different matter is the lovely little stainless pricking-out fork in the photo *above left*. This is the ideal present for someone who enjoys raising his

plants from seed, and it will last a lifetime. The garden-knife in the photo *below* is specially handy for tying-up operations. The end of a ball of garden twine is pulled through the knife along a special channel. As much twine as is needed for tying-up is pulled out. The remainder is snipped off with the knife, which remains attached to the twine.

Above right is a handy trowel with markings indicating the depth to which it has penetrated the soil. This is especially useful when planting bulbs. *Below* this is a beautiful stainless steel fork, which almost certainly will last you the rest of your life, even if you are only 20 now.

If your garden is fairly large, it's a nuisance to have to walk to the shed for every piece of equipment you want to use. To save this waste of time a special stand has been placed on this wheelbarrow, so that the most frequently used garden tools can easily be taken round the garden with you. The barrow can still be used in the ordinary way.
For older people, kneeling and straightening up is sometimes difficult. Hence this foldable kneeling-bench,

use on clayey soil. Both exist in rustproof form.
The Moisture Meter *below* is handy for people who don't know precisely when they ought to water. The pointer shows exactly whether the soil is wet, moist or dry. The apparatus must not be left outside.

rustproof and equipped with a rubber mat and space for small tools. Not a bad buy, but only obtainable so far in England.
The tool shown *above right* is a small hand-hoe with a wavy blade. It is designed to do all those hoeing jobs which an ordinary hoe cannot manage. There is also a small hand-mattock for

A terrace of wood

In many cases a terrace of wood can give a special atmosphere to your garden. It is often less expensive than a paved terrace, and differences of level are very easy to introduce. The best woods to use for these terraces are tropical hardwoods. The advantage over native woods is that tropical hardwood does not have to keep being impregnated, and it has tremendous durability. The way some of the hardwood weather to grey also creates a peaceful scene. One of the most important aspects of creating such a terrace is to obtain the correct proportions between the length, breadth and width of the parts, and of the chinks between the slats. The photo shows a good example. Great care is necessary in the construction. The drawing shows you how a terrace may be constructed. Concrete piles are set in the ground to the exact depth required. Beams are fastened to the heads of these

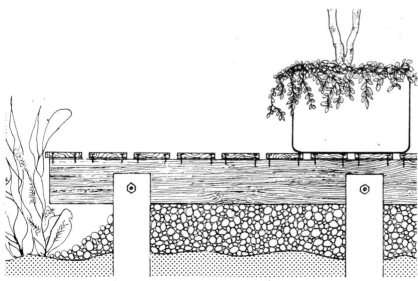

piles with bolts, there being the possibility of adjustment by a few centimetres if need be. The floorboards are attached to these beams by means of brass screws set in sunken holes. The vacant space under the terrace can best be filled up with a thick layer of coarse gravel.

Children in the garden

It is still exceptional if, when a garden is being planned, any thought is given to the fact that, if there are children in the family, they and their friends will want to play there too. Yet for the young child (6–10 years) the garden

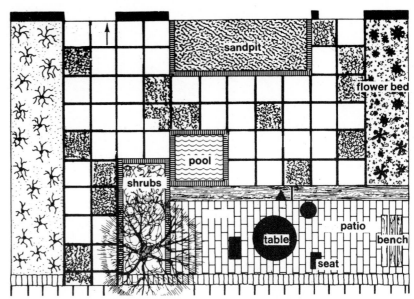

offers a whole world of possibilities for playing, undisturbed, unmolested, safe and private.

With gardens growing smaller, the possibilities of what one can provide for children to play on become more limited. It is seldom possible to supply a separate little area for the children and even the obligatory swing often has to

go, it spoils any garden with its obtrusive presence. Only the sandpit still occupies an important place, though often in an impractical form. Fortunately, many new play things, several of which are shown on the following pages, have been invented in recent years. Better, however, than any or all of these is to have the whole garden so laid out that it speaks to the imagination of the child, so that he sees in it rooms, little open squares and hidden spots, which stimulate play in a natural manner. From this point of view it is precisely the smaller, modern paved garden, with its differences of level, its little nooks, its varied plants and crazy paving, that is most stimulating to the smaller child.

A good sandpit is not difficult to make, yet for the most part one sees impractical, badly positioned ones, which ought to make every father of a family, sitting comfortably inside the house listening to his expensive stereo, feel ashamed. A really good sandpit should be built *in* the ground not on it, and surrounded with a rim of tiles on at least two sides. Then any spilled sand

can easily be swept back again.

The box is best situated in a place where mother can keep an eye on her little ones, and where there is some protection from sun and wind.

The large photograph shows a well planned sandpit. It is not difficult to site both sandpit and terrace or sunken

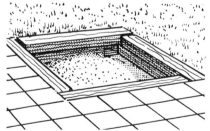

garden harmoniously, if only one is willing to take a little trouble over it. If cats are likely to come into the garden, the sandpit should have a hinged slatted or wire netting cover, which will let water through (otherwise the sand gets too dry) but keep out cats. A safeguard against the lid's falling is necessary. The plan shows how a sandpit can be sited in a sunken garden. A sandpit of the kind shown here can very easily be made out of two layers of old railway sleepers, the top ones sawn to measure. The corners are joined with long nails. For the balconies of flats and for very small gardens there are also plastic or fibreglass sand-tubs (*far right*).

An enormous variety of exciting garden playthings can be made from wood. It lasts longer and does not fall out of favour with children as quickly as plastic alternatives. At the back of a larger garden there is sometimes a good place for making a playhouse. The pyramid house (*below*) is very easy to make: to a child it is a climbing frame, a wigwam, a home – even perhaps a castle.

If there is sufficient space, a bowling-alley (*above*) can be made. If this is sunk and supported by wooden rims then the maintenance is unnecessary. Washable panels of stone or plastic are tremendously popular with the children for drawing on (*below*).

The plastic jungle made of plastic tubes can serve both as a decoration and as a piece of play apparatus (*above*).

A giant chessboard (*below*) is very easy to make. The tiles are usually 50×50 cm, but 30×30 cm will also do. One can buy the pieces or make them oneself.

Mobile gardens

You can use flower-pots and tubs not only for summer flowers of every kind, but also for fairly large trees, bushes, roses and perennials. Obviously, one needs pretty large containers for this purpose, yet even so the containers are often smaller than one might expect – 30 × 30 cm is large enough for a rose, 40 × 40 × 40 cm is suitable for a small tree or bush, while 50 × 50 × 50 cm is a good size for a 4 m high birch. Container gardening is rapidly increasing in popularity, not only for the balconies of flats but also for patios, where it is sometimes an advantage to be able to move a plant easily.

On the *opposite* page you see a fine example of trees in tubs, in this case fairly costly polyester receptacles. The photo series shows you how to set about it. *Above left* is a general view of the materials: the container or tub, a few sacks of special peatsoil, a barrow full of garden soil, a spade, and the tree (in this case an *Aralia*). See that the tub has good drainage-holes and place a few large crocks over them. Then begin to fill the tub: in turn a few spadefuls of special compost and garden soil. Mix everything thoroughly with the spade (*below left*). When the tub is ⅔ full, give it a thorough watering. Finally plant the tree so that the trunk is at the normal depth in the compost. Cover the clump with earth and press it all down very firmly.

On pages 81 and 82 you see examples of stone troughs, filled with rockplants. Old sinks are sometimes used for this purpose, as shown on page 82. In the photo *below* a feeding-trough is used. You can also have 'new' troughs made by a stone-mason.

Because rockplants will not tolerate standing water at the roots, the bottom must be drilled through, preferably in several places to ensure really good drainage. The bottom should then be covered with a good thick layer of coarse crocks or pebbles. The next step is to fill the trough with a growing compost such as John Innes potting compost No. 1, or a mixture of equal parts by volume of peat, soil and sand. For lime-loving plants a little lime should be added.

Next, place a few stones in the trough, set the rockplants, and sprinkle the surface with fine gravel or basalt chippings.

In winter cover the trough with a pane of glass to keep off excessive moisture. In summer water regularly but not too frequently, merely making sure that the soil in the troughs never dries out.

The idea that plants must be grown in the open ground in order to thrive is clearly disproved by the photo *right*. In this garden there is actually nothing growing in the ground itself. The depth in the earth of the luxuriant plantation alongside the garage path can be judged from the height of the concrete slabs – at the most 40 cm. The *Rhus* (*rear left*) is growing in a perfectly ordinary way in a box made of four washed concrete slabs. *Below* is an elegant English container, planted with tulips in the spring. *Below right* is a detail of a trough with rockplants. More of these on the next page.

The general view *adjacent* gives a good impression of the special 'garden of troughs' in the Royal Horticultural Society's gardens at Wisley. As you see, it is even possible to have small conifers thriving in troughs. *Below* you see a special roof-garden, constructed entirely of wood. To check rot, the wood has been impregnated under pressure, with a preservative that also darkens the wood. All the plants grow in pure peat, but need regular feeding and mulching. It constantly surprises me how well dark wood harmonizes with plants. Naturally, this example opens up prospects for your garden, for a roof-garden or balcony. If you are at all handy, you can easily build a wooden garden like this yourself. In the small trough *right*, the plants are growing in a mixture of sand and fertilized peat.

A garden of flowers for cutting

One of the great joys of gardening is that you can easily provide so much material for flower arrangements. There's no need for a great armful of blooms: with a few simple flowers, some attractive containers and foliage are all you need to make a stunning arrangement. Not all garden plants are good producers of flowers for cutting. And those that are, often grow too untidily to use in the border, and often look ugly after flowering. What better then than to make a special garden of flowers grown just for cutting – what the Victorians called a reserve garden. There the overhanging stems won't be in the way, and there one can also quite happily

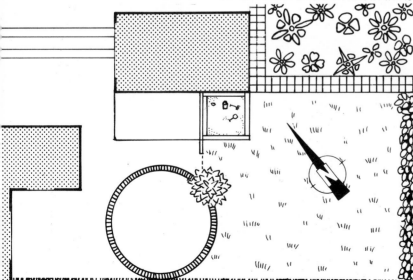

drive in a few sturdy stakes with wire or coarse-meshed netting stretched horizontally between, so that the stems can grow through and at the same time have support.

On the ground-plan you can see how such a cutflower garden could be sited, in this case half hidden behind a shed. The plot is sheltered from cold winds yet gets full sunshine, which is a necessity for most cut flowers. From these 15 square metres one can gather flowers all year long. There is a choice of tuberous plants (such as dahlias, gladioli), perennials (too numerous to mention) and annuals sown from seed (also a great assortment). On the following page you will see a few beautiful cut flowers in colour.

Many border plants can also provide
flowers for cutting. If the flowers are
taken from the borders, then the flowers
grown for cutting should be planted in
big, bold clumps.
Above left: Iris germanica hybrid
'*Stepping Out*'. *Below left* the warm
yellow of Helenium '*Wyndley*'. *Above*
another lovely iris: '*Rippling Waters*'.

Ponds

Almost every garden gains by the introduction of water in the form of a pond or stream. The mere presence of water has a peculiarly restful effect on most people, and this is just as important as having a garden that is stimulating and full of colour. The ideal place for the pond is on or close to the patio, because pondlife is fascinating to watch. The sound of water, particularly if there is a stream or fountain, contributes enormously to the garden-atmosphere: this natural murmuring and splashing is calming enough to make one forget the noise of traffic.

It does not matter whether the pond is large or small; that is just a question of relating the size of the pond to the size of the garden – to the size of your purse. What does matter is that the pond should be permanent (and therefore well constructed) and full of both fish and plants.

Pretty well all garden ponds are artificial, and very few are even fed by natural springs or streams. Plainly, in order to prevent the water from simply soaking away into the ground, some sort of impermeable structure must be built. This can consist of asphalt paper, plastic sheeting, concrete, brickwork or polyester. Large. picturesque ponds, as in the photo *right*, are sealed with foil or bitumen (asphalt), but smaller ponds are mostly of concrete (if made during the building of the house), or of polyester (if they are a later addition). The water in the pond must be nutritionally *poor*. If it is off mains water it will be nutritionally rather rich. This will result in your having a thick algae soup instead of clear pond water. The

algae feed on the salts in the tapwater. One can combat these algae by putting water-fleas in the pond. These will feed on the algae. Then the fish are put in, and they eat the fleas and their larvae. A food-chain is thus established which will keep the pond water clean. As soon as mains water is added, the water will become unbalanced again. With

rainwater there are usually no problems. Pondwater must also contain sufficient oxygen, and this is provided by various waterplants, especially water-thyme and pointed duckweed. The fish benefit from this oxygen. This should supply enough oxygen for them so long as not more than 2 or 3 moderately large fishes are allowed per square metre.

It is important that the pond is made deep enough to accommodate both fish and waterplants. The minimum useful depth is 60 cm. In winter a hole must be made in ice. This is most easily done by leaving a ball floating on the surface: when the water freezes remove the ball: replace it again before nightfall. Do *not* knock a hole in the ice: it could concuss the fish and kill them.

Most waterplants are plants of the
riverbank and marshes; they like a water
depth of from 0–20 cm. This is difficult
to bring into accord with the minimum
pond-depth of 60 cm. The ideal small
pond has the form as shown in the
drawing. In the middle, the depth is
60 cm (or more). Here the fish can take
refuge in really cold weather. It can also
be used to grow waterlilies, which like to
stand in deeper water. The sides of the
pond have a depth of only 30 cm. By
placing plant containers on this shelf and
standing the containers on bricks, the
exact desired planting-depth can be
reached. Ponds of this kind, made of
polyester or fibreglass can be bought
ready-made round, rectangular or
irregular in shape. The pond on page 89
is one of these, shown in its setting. You
can see it even better on page 90. There
are various methods of screening the
edge of the pond, as the drawing shows.
On this page several practical examples
are illustrated.
Right the bank of a larger pond,
gradually sloping. The stones rest on a
bed of puddled clay, which keeps the
pond watertight.

Above left An old stone horse-trough, set on top of some outsize pebbles, makes a striking feature in this garden. *Above right* a simple round pond with sprinkler. *Below left* a similar pond standing up above its surroundings. *Below right* stepping-stones always create a pleasing effect.

Polystyrene containers are ideal for growing plants in ponds. They should be filled with a mixture of clay and peat, which is then thoroughly moistened. Waterlilies are planted in shallow, square boxes (*below*). After planting, the surface of the soil is covered in a thin layer of sharp sand, to prevent clay particles fouling the pond water. Finally the whole box is placed carefully in the deepest part (*far below*). The bankside plants can be placed in narrow polystyrene balcony-boxes (*right*), although it is better to use somewhat wider containers, to give the roots more room.

To the *right* is an example of the type of pump that can be placed in its entirety in the pond and used to drive a fountain. See also the drawing on page 87. The flex is laid in an inconspicuous position along the edge. Different fountain patterns can be obtained by using different nozzles.

Tying up

Many plants require a certain amount of help to keep upright, especially of course climbers, of which only a very small number like ivy *Hedera* and Virginia creeper *Parthenocissus* are self-clinging. By far the most satisfactory system of supporting climbers is to take a masonry drill and make a good number of holes in the wall (*above left*) and then knock plastic wall-plugs into these (*above centre*). Brass eye-screws can then be screwed into them. These last forever and are scarcely noticeable. The stems can then be fastened with string or plastic-covered wire (*above right*). There are also paper fastening-strips with an interior wire thread designed for tying up plants. These are worthless because the paper comes off and the thin wire cuts into the plant. Similar strips made of plastic are much better. For thicker stems there are many sorts of plastic strips with perforations. Tying up perennials is also very important. There

are two methods. *Below left* tying with the aid of bamboo canes and garden twine. Take care that the plants are not tied too tightly. *Below right* supporting with twigs. Suitable branches are placed among the perennials early in spring so that they can then grow up through them.

Combinations

The secret of a garden's atmosphere lies to a great extent in finding the right combinations of colour. In this, stones, walls and other materials in the surroundings play as much of a part as the plants themselves. To the *right* is a good example of contrast in form and colour: *Phlox paniculata* with *Veronica*. The photo *below* shows *Phlox* in another tint, this time in combination with *Achillea filipendulina*.
Page 93 shows *Aruncus dioicus* (white) with *Campanula latifolia* 'Macrantha'.

Watering

Why does one have to water the garden? After all, in nature there are no little gnomes with garden-hose at the ready, yet everything turns out splendidly. On the other hand there are differences. Garden conditions cannot be compared with natural circumstances. Of the plants we grow 90% are not natives. They need extra care. We cut the grass so short that it is almost *bound* to wither, and yet we expect it to be fresh and green. It is precisely on this account that a garden-sprinkler is such an indispensable instrument.

It is worth giving some thought to the water we use in the garden. Mains water is always inferior; it usually contains a lot of lime and chemicals which are more or less poisonous to many plants. Heathers, rhododendrons and conifers in particular are decidedly not very fond of it. This does not alter the basic fact that bad water is often a lot better than no water at all. Of course, if your garden borders on a ditch or canal, with good old-fashioned water streaming through (unpolluted by industry) then you can

profitably use an electric pump (*small photo*) which has a considerable water-displacement and can always provide more water than the tap. Rainwater collected in a large butt is the next best alternative.

Water meets with resistance in its journey through pipes, taps and hoses, and the pressure gradually decreases. The longer and narrower the hose-pipe, and the more joins there are in it, the more the pressure will decrease. For this reason a simple hose run off an ordinary tap is by far the most effective.

It is also noticeable that when the whole neighbourhood is busy watering pressure drops rapidly and only a pitiful little dribble comes out of the nozzle or sprinkler. When this happens it is best to set the sprinkler, and then wait till your neighbours have finished watering before turning yours on – even if it is after dark. As a rule, a $\frac{1}{2}''$ hose is used in the garden. The more expensive, reinforced plastic hose is a much better buy than the rather thin PVC hose which is more commonly bought. It does not crack, and is far longer-lasting. For hoses longer than 25 m you should use $\frac{5}{8}''$ or $\frac{3}{4}''$ diameter hose, then you will lose less pressure.

It is often claimed that watering in the sunshine, as in the photo *above*, is wrong. The droplets are supposed to cause scorching of the plants. This is not so.

Besides, if you water in the heat of the day the water gets warmed on its way through the hose and in the air and your plants don't get such a 'shock' from the cold water. Furthermore, the water-pressure is usually much better during the day and you'll get the job done quicker – unless you want to wait till after dark. How do you diagnose when the garden needs watering? The lawn generally gives the first indication. It starts turning slightly yellowish. Water directly, doing the lawn first and then the borders. Remember always that a good soaking that keeps the ground wet for a week is far more use than a little water sprinkled on the surface that never has a chance to soak right down into the soil – which is where it is needed, by the roots.

The connecting of tap, hose and sprinkler by means of hose-columns, coupling-nuts, clamps and jubilee clips is now fortunately completely out of date. Far more efficient are the modern high-speed plastic connectors. These have brought about a revolution in watering technology. There are various makes but

only two basic styles: with or without a waterstop. Without the stop you get a lively water ballet when you change one fitting for another without first turning off the tap (*above left*). If there is a waterstop in the connector, then you save yourself this soaking (*above right*). A waterstop does cause some loss of pressure, and should only be used at the end of the hose.

Attaching the hose to the connector is simplicity itself. Just press the connector on to its counterpart, and twist the locking cap till it is tight (*far left*). If all the pieces of hose are provided with connectors, then you can if you wish make watertight connections with two-

and threeway pieces (*centre left and right*).

In the United States all sprinklers and other aids are fitted with $\frac{3}{4}''$ American thread, which unfortunately does not correspond to the $\frac{3}{4}''$ European pipe-thread, which is found in our taps (or most of them, at any rate) and aids. To make the conversion possible, there are various connectors and reducers, as in the photo (*right*). For the usual sizes ($\frac{1}{4}''$, $\frac{1}{2}''$, $\frac{3}{4}''$ and $1''$ European thread and $\frac{3}{4}''$ American thread) there are direct connecting-pieces, so that the reducing-rings (second row from the top) are not so often needed. Ask your supplier for a catalogue.

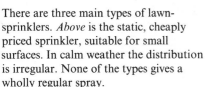

There are three main types of lawn-sprinklers. *Above* is the static, cheaply priced sprinkler, suitable for small surfaces. In calm weather the distribution is irregular. None of the types gives a wholly regular spray.
This rotating sprinkler covers a larger area and gives a better water-distribution. Flow-resistance is slight,

resulting in a high yield per unit of time. *Above right* is the square or oscillating-sprinkler, the type that is most suitable for somewhat larger gardens. Unfortunately, the arm as a rule stays too long in the outermost position (though not in the model illustrated), with the result that relatively little water

falls in the middle of the square being watered.
Below right is a sprinkler-hose, a specially perforated hose that works very well so long as the very fine holes do not become clogged with dirt or blocked by lice or centipedes which seem to like hiding in hoses.

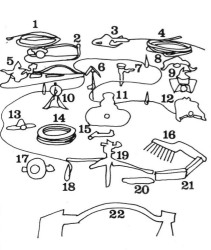

1 Nobel sprinkling-hose. *2* Wolf WQ oscillating sprinkler. *3* Melnor 860 rotating sprinkler. *4* Reinforced hose with Wolf connector. *5* Far-reach Wolf WR. *6* KYM rotating sprinkler. *7* Wolf WN 4-way sprinkler. *8* Melnor 910 adjustable rotating sprinkler. *9* Wolf WP rotating sprinkler. *10* HECO butterfly-sprinkler. *11* Pulsating 3-way sprinkler Melnor 1540. *12* 4-way plateau-sprinkler Melnor 685. *13* KYM fixed sprinkler. *14* Allen fixed sprinkler. *15* Melnor 425C sprinkle-pistol. *16* Wolf XK 24 auto-brush. *17* Melnor 100 water-timer. *18* Fonteina sprinkling-set. *19* Naan 413 pulsating sprinkler. *20* Wolf XK 11 garden syringe. *21* Wolf XK 18 hand-shower. *22* Far-reach Melnor 725.

The area covered by the sprinkler depends largely on the type. The simple static and rotating sprinklers (previous page, *above left and centre*) always water a circular area. Since a garden is seldom round, this means that the corners get no water.

The water-distribution of the rain- or oscillating-sprinklers is more satisfactory. The perforated arm swings slowly to and fro, sweeping over a rectangular area as it does so. Moreover, most models can be adjusted to water only the area to the left or right of the sprinkler, the middle area, or the whole surface. The diagram illustrates this, and *above* it is a photo of the adjustment knob. Some rotating sprinklers can work in segments, as does the pulsating sprinkler to the *right*. The various positions are shown in the diagram *below* the photo.

The oscillating-sprinkler shown on page 99, *far right* can if so wished also

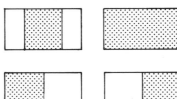

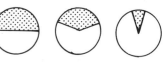

produce a shorter range of jets, in which case it covers a narrower rectangle.

The mobile sprinkler (*left*) extends the hose to its full length and then slowly winds itself back in its tracks, automatically winding up the hose and watering as it goes. It waters quite a large area (see diagram).

To maintain sufficient pressure, not more than 25 m of hose should be used.

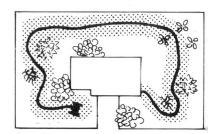

On this page are a few more sprinklers of different types. *Above left*, a rotating sprinkler made entirely of plastic. The base fills with water, the weight of which keeps the sprinkler steady. *Below this* is a de luxe rotating model: the nozzles are adjustable, so that not only the type of jet but also the speed of rotation can be regulated and the sprinkler can even be slowed down to a standstill.

Above centre is a sprinkler with a rotating platform upon which there are four different types of nozzles. One can select which one of these one wants to use. *Below this* is an oscillating sprinkler with a free arm. The construction is such that the width of the array of jets can be varied. They can even be adjusted so that the jets disappear and a fine mist is formed (*above right*).

Below left is a fairly primitive but highly effective arrangement for checking just how a particular sprinkler distributes the water. At every 50 cm from the sprinkler, a plastic cup is placed. After a certain time the quantity of water in each cup is measured. An instructive test, which shows that there is not a single sprinkler on the market which gives an absolutely regular distribution of water. You need to know where most water falls with your particular sprinkler so that you can re-water those areas which receive relatively little of the spray.

Watering, of course, does not have to take place from a fixed position. Indeed, it is often handier to have portable aids at your disposal. The watering-can is completely independent of the mains supply, and is easily filled from a garden tap or rainwater butt. *Right* you see a superior English model with a non-corrosive brass hose which gives a very fine spray. The can itself is made of galvanized steel. These are preferable to plastic watering-cans, but are somewhat heavier of course.

Below is a practical hand-shower, ideal for watering isolated seed-boxes and beds. It is quick to put on or take off, fits directly on to the high-speed connecting system and is provided with a regulator stop-tap.

Above right is a water-pistol for grown ups. With trigger released no water flows at all. If you squeeze the handle a little you get a wide spray of mist, if you press harder you get a straight jet (*second photo*).

With the all-plastic sprinkler (*third from the top*) you change the shape of the jet, by turning the head of the nozzle. This too, fits directly on the rapid-connectors.

Right bottom is a very important but often forgotten part of garden-sprinklers: the filter. This can soon get blocked up by algae, so it is wise to take it out and clean it frequently. The sprinkler will then do its work much better.

Of the remaining watering aids, the hose reel, on which the hose itself can be neatly wound up and stored, is probably the most important. If you buy a good strong model, with a reinforced hose and good connectors, then the tap can be left on all the time. Most useful of all are the reels that can be mounted on a wall (*photograph below*). They can be mounted at a convenient height for winding up the hose.

Separate stop-cocks can be handy as

further aids. They are provided with American $\frac{3}{4}''$ thread, and can be adapted to fit on the sprinkler and connecting-system already mentioned (*below centre*). The water-timer (*below right*) is extremely useful. It works just like a water-meter. You set if for a

quantity of, for example, 3000 litres of water; as soon as this has passed, the device cuts off the supply. The clock above is available as a separate item; the one below is built-in to the Melnor oscillating-sprinkler.

101

In larger gardens it is useful to have more than one point from which water can be drawn. Extra points can be provided quite simply by making use of reinforced plastic hose, preferably ¾″, and burying it in trenches in the ground where it can stay permanently. Branch-lines can be made by using three-way junctions and high-speed plastic connectors. The system is flexible in layout and can always be removed. The hose should be buried at least a foot deep (*below centre*).

Tap-points can be made very easily by pushing a piece of plastic pipe of suitable size into the ground, inserting the underground hose from the side, and providing the end of the hose with a

connector with a waterstop (large photo). The garden-sprinkler is run off a ½″ hose connected to the point by means of a 'stopcontact', a device which switches off the water the moment the connection is broken (*far left*). The plastic contact box (*far right*) can be buried in the ground with the lid at soil level.

102

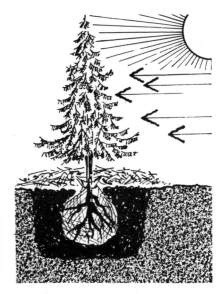

Planting conifers

Conifers are best planted in April–May, or else in August. Autumn planting is not advisable because the cold winter winds dehydrates the trees before their roots have become established (diagram *above right*). When you buy conifers, make sure that they have a good firm ball of soil round the roots (*above left*). If the ball of soil has dried out at the garden centre or nursery, stand the plant in a bucket of water and give it a good, long drink (*above centre*). Only when you have set the plant in enriched, preferably peatish garden soil, should the mesh bag in which the root-ball is contained be unknotted or cut loose (*below left*). Fold it outwards, but do not attempt to remove it. Fill in with peat round the stem, and then give another good watering. Finally, fill in with more earth and tread down, taking care that the conifer is standing upright all the time (*below right*).

Lawns

In most gardens the lawn occupies an important, central place. Since there are different kinds of lawn, it is useful to consider which type is best suited to your garden. The *ornamental lawn* consists of very fine sorts of grass, which are referred to in the trade as English or classic mixture (see also further on). These grasses form a particularly homogeneous carpet and require relatively little mowing. Their resistance to being walked upon is not however very great, and such lawns will not withstand hard wear. The *utility lawn* is based on a mixture of grasses used for sports fields. The grasses found in it are much coarser, so it looks less beautiful. Growth is more rapid, especially when rye-grass is included in the mixture. Its advantage is that it has a much greater resistance to treading, and that bare patches grow over much sooner.

The *surface* of your lawn depends on your choice of grass-mixture. Since small lawns get walked over relatively more than large ones, 5×5 m is almost too small for an ornamental lawn, unless one scarcely ever walks or sits on it. On the other hand, a 20×80 m lawn can cheerfully be played on by children, even if it is sown with an English mixture. In some gardens it is possible to make *two lawns*: a play-lawn, clearly separated in the layout of buildings from the ornamental lawn, which lies more in the direct view from the house.

The most important varieties of grass for lawns are: Chewing's Fescue, Browntop Bent, Crested Dogstail, Smooth-stalked Meadow grass and Rye-grass. The first two types are used for purely ornamental lawns, the last two are pre-eminently suitable for the play-lawn. Grass varieties such as Heathgrass and Fine-leaved Sheep-grass, are employed only exceptionally.

Mixtures of two or more grass-varieties are in general the most useful since there are various grass-diseases which can destroy a particular kind of grass. If one sows a mixture, then at least one sort will survive. Which one survives is also partly determined by the amount of treading and especially by the acid-content of the soil. Thus in acid soils, out of the classic mixture 20% Browntop Bent and 80% Red Fescue grass, after a few years only the Browntop Bent will remain. On the other hand, if one lives on clay then it will be the Red Fescue that survives. The hardy mixtures for play-lawns, consisting of Crested Dogstail, Browntop Bent and Rye-grass, with perhaps the addition of some Red Fescue and Timothy, require a soil with not too low a pH (about 6 to 7).

The *buying* of good grass-seed is a question of trust, because the packet does not always give sufficient information on the seed mixture inside. Most of the seed firms whose names are household words offer mixtures for various purposes. These can be relied upon completely.

Many lawns are made by laying turves. This has the advantage of providing almost instant lawn. Provided the turves are fresh they will quickly form a good sward. The disadvantage of forming a lawn from turf is that you don't know where the turf has come from, and you don't know which sorts of grasses it is composed of. Some turves are specially raised from lawn mixtures, but the majority are simply taken from an old meadow. If properly laid and treated with selective weedkillers and lawn-fertilizers these will make excellent lawns in time.

Weeds in the lawn can be combated with selective herbicides which will destroy most of the broad-leaved weeds like daisies and dandelions. If you use a weedkiller on the lawn you should also feed it to encourage the grass to grow into the spaces left by the weeds. Most weedkillers are highly poisonous and great care should be taken when handling them.

A weed that can't be tackled chemically is *Poa annua*, a coarse-growing annual grass. The result is that practically all lawns consist of a very large part of this weed. Only when one is constantly on the alert and weeds out turfs of *Poa annua* by hand (see photo) can lawns be kept free from it. Later on, providing the lawn is tightly grown and kept in perfect condition, *Poa annua* will not find it so easy to establish itself.

A mown lawn cannot really thrive in the *shade*. Lack of light impedes metabolism in short little leaf-blades. If one cuts the grass higher under trees, so much the better; if one leaves it unmown, then there is no problem. A better alternative is usually to make beds under the trees and fill them with ground-cover plants.

The *mowing-height* is a point that deserves much attention. Ornamental lawns are best cut $1\frac{1}{2}$ to 2 cm above the ground. A lawn meant for use, grown from a mixture containing Crested Dogstail, Browntop Bent and Rye-grass, should not however be cut shorter than 4 cm, because if it is the grass cannot develop enough resistance to weeds. Finally, as for *frequency of mowing*, a

lawn needs to be cut at least once a week from March till October to look even passable. If you want it to look positively marvellous it should be cut twice a week from the beginning of May till the end of September – but that is perhaps a counsel of perfection.

The *sowing* of a new lawn is best done at the end of August. This is usually a moist, fairly warm period, and is therefore ideal for the germination of the seeds. It gets the new grass off to a really good start. The end of April is also a good time to sow, but this rather depends on the weather. There is also a technique for sowing grass throughout the summer, but more on this later.

The clearing and levelling of the ground should start 2½ months before you want to sow the seed. The first step is to dig the ground. The standard method is shown on this page. If an existing lawn is being reconstructed, first take out a trench the width of the spade. The excavated soil should be carried away and kept: it will be needed later on. Then make the second trench, first cutting off the turf (*above*) and laying it upside down in the trench you have just made. Next, dig out the soil from the second trench and throw it on top of the upturned turves. Continue in this way, each successive trench filling the previous one, until the whole area is prepared (see also diagram).

If ground which has been lying fallow is to be transformed into a lawn, it may be necessary to follow a different digging procedure. For more details see pages 130–135 inclusive.

It is very important that after digging the whole surface should be trodden down with the heels (*below left*). This is the

best method of finding out soft patches in the sub-soil. These can then be filled and levelled.

After treading-in the lawn must be left as it is for at least two months. This is very important, for it gives the weed-seeds, abundantly present in almost every soil, the chance to germinate. Once they come through you can get rid of them either by hoeing (in dry weather) or by spraying with Paraquat. Do not, however, disturb the soil any deeper than 2 cm, otherwise you'll bring fresh weed-seeds to the surface.

Just before sowing the soil should finally be very lightly raked to make it even (*below right*).

Because grass-seed as a rule consists of a mixture of two or more varieties, it is

important to mix it up very thoroughly (page 107, *above left*). Often a little clean white sand is added, which is easier to scatter. Then the sowing can begin (page 107, *above centre*).

It is best to sow a new lawn as thinly as possible, first breadthwise, then lengthwise and, if there is any seed left, breadthwise again.

very poor in this case, too.

In order to allow germination to proceed well under all circumstances, you can mix peat into the topmost 2 to 3 cm of soil, at the rate of 1 cubic metre per hundred square metres of lawn. That is a layer about 1 cm thick. If this is mixed into the top 2 cm of soil, you will finish up with a lawn seedbed of which the peat makes up 30 to 50%.

You can then confidently give a daily watering, since the peat will not become compacted.

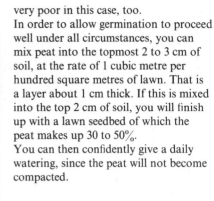

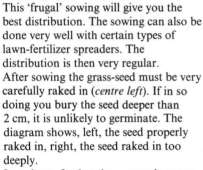

This 'frugal' sowing will give you the best distribution. The sowing can also be done very well with certain types of lawn-fertilizer spreaders. The distribution is then very regular.

After sowing the grass-seed must be very carefully raked in (*centre left*). If in so doing you bury the seed deeper than 2 cm, it is unlikely to germinate. The diagram shows, left, the seed properly raked in, right, the seed raked in too deeply.

In order to further the contact between seed and soil, it is useful to tread the whole surface with little planks, or to go over it with the garden roller (page 108, *left*).

For grass-seed to germinate three things are needed: warmth, moisture and air. Over the first factor you have little control except to sow at the right season, but a lack of moisture soon occurs in the topmost layer of soil. This is not serious so long as the seed is still dormant, but it is disastrous if the seed has already begun to sprout. What happens is that the embryo dries up. If you set about watering the garden soil will become tightly compacted and then no air will get to the seeds and germination will be

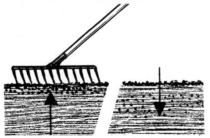

If the lawn is very big, or if you have difficulties in getting a correct distribution of grass-seed, you can set to work as indicated in the diagram on page 108. The seed and the lawn are divided up into the same number of equal portions and compartments. You sow one portion in each compartment.

107

Birds love grass-seed. They'll try to grab
it out of your hands as you sow it. The
best way to protect the embryo lawn is
by stretching a net or threads of black
yarn across it. Another excellent article
for this purpose is a sort of angels'-hair
or artificial cobweb made of fibreglass.
The artificial fibres can be pulled out to
great lengths. The network is fastened
round the edges with little sticks (*right*).
This is sure to keep the sparrows away
now. Keeping the sown area moist is also
an effective deterrent, but it is only
workable if you have used peat in the
soil. Water distributed like rain through
a perforated hose as shown on page 97
gives the finest spray and is best for the
germinating seeds.

There is an abundance of machines on the market for *mowing* the lawn – the only question is which type to buy for your particular purpose.

Lawn-mowers are divided into two types: rotary mowers which *cut down* the grass by means of a horizontally revolving blade, and cylinder mowers, which employ a set of rotating blades which *cut through* the grass by turning against a fixed bottom blade. For long or irregularly mown grass, rotary mowers are definitely best. Cylinder mowers are designed for those who want a really fine lawn. All hand-mowers are cylinder mowers. On the *far left* you see three rotary cutters, one above the other. The top one is petrol-driven, the one below is a 220 V mains-powered mower, and the machine at the bottom is an electric battery model.

The same distinctions apply to the cylinder mowers shown in the row to the right. Here again, from top to bottom, is a petrol-driven, a 220 V mains electric, and a battery-powered mower.

Finally, *far right below*, is a simple hand-mower. The size of the lawn, the amount of noise you will tolerate or are prepared to inflict on your neighbours and your own physical fitness, are all factors that will determine your choice. Undoubtedly a hand-mower gives the best results, but that may not always be the main consideration. Electric mowers are quietest, though the battery ones can only cope with small lawns.

Electrically powered mowers are quiet and emit no smelly fumes such as those you get from a petrol motor. A disadvantage of mains-powered machines, however, is the cable, which often gets in the way. The best way of getting to work is shown in the three photos *above*. *Left* is the outward

up and down the lawn (*centre right*). *Setting the height* at which the mower cuts is very important. In cylinder mowers this is generally done by adjusting the small support-roller (*left*). In more expensive machines the wheel-height is also changeable and can be done independently (*centre*). In this way

journey, with the cable hanging at the right side. On turning (*centre*) the cable also changes sides. It now hangs on the left side, and what is more lies on the *cut* grass. In this way you avoid mowing the cable – a dangerous thing to do to say the least.
Some mowers are fitted with self-winding cables that wind and unwind as you go

it is possible when cutting the edge of the lawn to have one wheel running on the soil and the other on the grass, with the machine still mowing. In rotary cutters the height of cut is altered by adjusting all four wheels. Sometimes this has to be done with a key, but there are also machines with an attached handle (*right*).

Grass collection can take place in various ways. The grass-rake (*right*) is very useful and can also be used for removing leaves in autumn. One disadvantage of the rake is that it combs up the little blades of grass and so eradicates the striped effect which the mower has so carefully created. A simple rake of bamboo is very light and easy to use. On the other hand the advantage of using a rake is that it will gather up some of the moss from the lawn.

The hopper (*below*) is an easier method of collecting the mowings and saves time, even if it does have to be emptied after every journey. The striped effect on the lawn remains. Rotary mowers too, can be provided with hoppers (*below left*).

For larger lawns a sweeping machine is useful (*below right*). Then there is also the garden suction-machine (page 70). During sunny weather in June–July it is better *not* to clear away the cuttings, and not to cut the grass so short. This gives the grass some protection and helps to prevent it from drying out so fast.

Trimming the edges of the lawn is almost superfluous if you design your garden so that your lawn is bounded by tiles or stones, over which the mower can ride. There are examples of how this may be done throughout the book, but see particularly the pictures on pages 26 and 53. If you have done this then you have also largely eliminated edge-trimming. All one need do is touch up the flat-

trodden grass from time to time. If you don't like this type of design and enjoy the edging chore, then there is a wide choice of tools for the job. *Far left* the edge-cutter, to be used only a few times a year. *Above left* the very practical edging-shear with long arms. *Below this* a very good electrical shear, working from a built-in battery. *At the bottom* an edging-shear that can be used vertically or horizontally. *Above right* a rotating edge-trimmer, which is pushed forward with a long handle.

It is worth remembering that if you do have edges to the lawn, they will not remain straight, but tend to warp and twist. This means that you will periodically need to use an edging tool to straighten them up again, using a board to get a straight line.

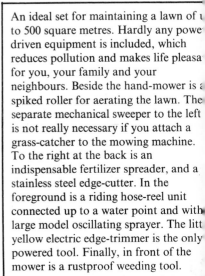

An ideal set for maintaining a lawn of up to 500 square metres. Hardly any power driven equipment is included, which reduces pollution and makes life pleasant for you, your family and your neighbours. Beside the hand-mower is a spiked roller for aerating the lawn. The separate mechanical sweeper to the left is not really necessary if you attach a grass-catcher to the mowing machine. To the right at the back is an indispensable fertilizer spreader, and a stainless steel edge-cutter. In the foreground is a riding hose-reel unit connected up to a water point and with a large model oscillating sprayer. The little yellow electric edge-trimmer is the only powered tool. Finally, in front of the mower is a rustproof weeding tool.

There are numerous devices on the market which you can use for aerating the lawn. Most of them are good and many are shown on this page.

The *aeration* or pricking of the lawn is enormously important. The more a lawn is trodden (or mown) the more the upper layer becomes compacted: the grass-roots start to wither and moss gains the upper hand. Aerators penetrate this compacted layer and let the lawn 'breathe' again. The work of aerating the lawn must be done several times a year, beginning in April. It often precedes the dressing of the lawn (next page) and accompanies the fertilizing (see page 15).

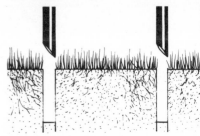

Top left is a simple hand-held spiker, with solid tines.

Top right is a better spiker with hollow tines and springs. The diagram underneath shows the result in cross-section. The holes can later be filled with sharp sand, then the little channels remain in function for a long time.

Centre left is a rubber lawn-comb, only for very superficial aeration. The moss rake, shown *centre*, works better. Narrow steel blades slit through the turf.

Centre right a rotating spiker for lawns of average size. Simple but effective are the spikes (*below left*) that you can strap on to your shoes and aerate the lawn as you mow it.

The main purpose of dressing a lawn is to keep it level (see diagram). It is sufficient to do this once a year, preferably in June. There are various products on the market for dressing lawns, but one of the best combinations is peat (*left*) and compost (*right*). This gives a reasonably neutral mixture. After mixing, scatter the dressing over the lawn (*above*). This is best done during dry weather. Next, brush the dressing well in (*below left*), then water it in (*below right*). Coarse remnants, that won't go down among the grass, can be removed later. Apart from keeping the lawn level, dressing it also helps to feed it, and to add humus which keeps it soft and springy underfoot, as well as encouraging worms.

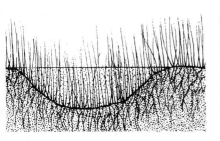

Whether you want a patch of greensward where the children can happily play, or an elegant, English lawn, you can, with a little care, maintain the lawn so that it will always look lovely and green. The smaller the lawn, the more care it will need, especially if you have children romping over it.

Greenhouses

An unheated greenhouse is very little use. If you leave plants inside for the winter they'll freeze to death – unless they are hardy enough to survive in the open garden anyway. So, when purchasing a greenhouse make sure you include a really satisfactory heating system. Buy only from a supplier who can provide all accessories, otherwise you could be in difficulties later on when you want to extend or add extra equipment. Think firstly about what you most want to grow in your greenhouse, and also consider how much time you will be able to devote to your new hobby. Orchids require a different type of greenhouse and a different form of heating from cacti, and also more time spent on them, to mention one example. Choose something to cultivate from which you can derive pleasure throughout the whole year.

Decide in advance which material you will choose: cedarwood, steel or aluminium. Cedarwood needs to be oiled every year; other woods need painting fairly frequently. Aluminium becomes ugly rather quickly in coastal regions. Ask yourself which is the best site for your greenhouse. As a rule a free-standing greenhouse is the best (*above*); if there happens to be a deciduous tree on the south side which casts light shade, that is quite useful. Sometimes a lean-to greenhouse (*bottom far right*) is the best solution. If you have little room, then a balcony-frame (*right*) might be preferable, especially for plants that remain small, such as cacti. Remember about keeping out the frost. Only in rather larger gardens will unusual forms (*top far right*) be much use.

118

Oil is a reliable source of heating if a substantial, thermostatically controlled stove is used, equipped with a stove-pipe and a ventilator to carry off fumes. In general all other types of oil-heaters should be avoided, especially the free-standing ones.

Gas is becoming very popular for greenhouse-heating. You can either use a hot-water system with a special geyser, as shown *above*, or a more conventional type of boiler. Be sure to choose a type that gives you complete thermostatic control.

Electricity will be needed in the greenhouse, even if only for lighting. Electric heating is best of all, and installation is not expensive. The running-cost is unfortunately somewhat high. At the *top* is a fan-heater, *below this* a tubular heater.

Ventilation is very important. Roof-windows are a necessity, side windows a luxury. A handy device is an automatic window-opener, which simply opens the windows when the temperature reaches a pre-set point. In practice one often forgets to ventilate, so such automatic aids are very useful. Some people prefer louvres or automatic fans to simple windows.

Shade is a necessity for all plants except succulents. In the large photo on page 118 is a greenhouse with a high-placed sun-excluder; this enables the windows to open underneath it. *Above* is a plastic roller-blind, *inside* the greenhouse. Best of all is a tree in just the right place. In summer one can also whiten the windows with a proprietary wash.

Outside snow may cover the garden, but in your greenhouse leafy tropical plants flourish unconcerned. That is one of the advantages of a heated greenhouse: it's a hobby you can enjoy all the year round (*left*).

If you do not have the space for a free-standing greenhouse, there are good lean-to models, such as the aluminium one on the *right*. Notice the green plastic blinds to shade the plants in summer. If buying a greenhouse is stretching your purse then a frame in which bedding-plants and the like can be raised is a good buy. With the aid of soil-warming cables you can even bring cacti through the winter in one of these (*below*).

Some people consider the automation of a domestic greenhouse an excessive luxury. They say it takes the skill out of greenhouse gardening. In fact few of us have time enough to spend the whole day attending to the greenhouse. Things can go badly wrong if there's nobody at home and the sun breaks through and everything is shut up tight. At times like this, automatic ventilation would save your plants.

In the same way, in one ice-cold night all your orchids could die of frost if the heating wasn't quite adequate and there was no emergency alarm to rouse your attention. This happens quite often to people who think such an investment a waste of money and an insult to their meterological acumen.

The real point of an automatic greenhouse is that you can enjoy the plants and forget the chores. You double the fun for half the effort and your plants are safe.

The plants will be grateful in any case, for they need only one thing: *regularity* in care. And that is precisely what automation gives.

expensive, and very useful, especially if you're sometimes away for long periods. *Below right* is a mist-spray which, in response to a hygroscope, automatically maintains the moisture in the air at fixed level. The large photo shows you an automated greenhouse, in which most of the devices we have discussed have been installed.

In the small photo *above left* is a thermostat for controlling the soil's temperature. It is normally only used in a propagating case, together with electric warming-cables. *Below left* are two ventilator-heaters with built-in thermostats. When these switch on they blow air gently all round the greenhouse. Air circulation is very important

Centre is a header tank for a capillary bench, giving automatic watering. Not

Planting bulbs

If you plant tulips in the same place year after year, sooner or later the soil will become 'sick'. There is a special powder to prevent this. The picture at the *top* shows you how a tulip-bed is planted: first the soil is dug out 7–10 cm deep, then the bulbs are pressed side by side into the loosened soil and sprinkled with the powder. The excavated soil is then put back again. The tulips are at the same depth, and will flower at the same time. The *adjacent* photo shows the planting of crocuses in a lawn. With a sharp spade cut out several turves, loosen the subsoil a little and press the bulbs in. Then put back the turves. You can then forget the crocuses till they surprise you in the spring. For planting small groups of bulbs the bulb-planter on the *right* is a very handy little tool. Stick it into the ground to the required depth; the soil stays inside; pop a bulb in the hole, and then tap the planter and the earth will fall back into place again. The drawing gives you another suggestion for the combined planting of perennials and flower-bulbs. Set the bulbs everywhere between the clumps in the autumn, then they will flower just as the perennials are beginning to come into flower, making a stunning display.

The composition of a mixed bed including spring-bulbs is something that is carried out in a completely different way in different countries. The English have found the best solution: they do not allow the bulbs to over-dominate, but plant them together with other spring flowers. The large photo *left* is an example of this style: a quite ordinary country garden in England, in which tulips are flowering together with fully-open daisies (*foreground*), yellow Wallflowers and light blue Forget-me-nots.

Right is an even more comprehensive combination, in which the tulips play a subordinate role. In the foreground are purple Aubretia and yellow Alyssum. Between the tulips are blue Forget-me-nots and yellow and orange Wallflowers. The wall is covered with Wistaria. Another pleasing combination is with Prunus. *Below* is a Dutch example, with a pink *Prunus nipponica* on the right. The combination *right* consists of *Tulipa violacea* and *Chionodoxa luciliae*.

Lighting

Garden lighting is generally placed in the lawn, so that from thence the borders and shrubs are illuminated from beneath. This gives a very dramatic effect, but the lamps and flexes can get in the way. For this reason it is sometimes

better to illuminate a garden (*above*) from above. The lamps, with the aid of an additional wall-plate, can be fixed below the eaves of house and garage (*above left*). On the plan you can see how the lamps were placed to light the garden in the big picture. They were 150 watt, 'flood' type lamps, hence with wide beam. Viewed from the room, the lamps were always hidden behind a wall or corner, so that they were not visible.

If you have an attractive garden into which you have put a lot of work, it's rather a pity when there is nothing of it to be seen in the evening especially if you enjoy barbecues on warm evenings. On

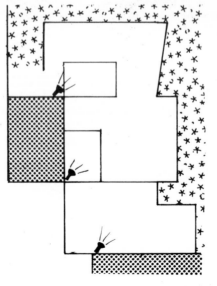

such occasions permanent garden lighting can turn the treacherous darkness of the garden into a veritable wonderland of light, shade and colour. Complete sets of garden lights are available, consisting of a fitting with moulded-on cable, contact stops and extension lead (*below left*). The fitting is drip-proof (can also be obtained completely watertight, for use in ponds) and all the rest is rubber. The only snag is the fixed length of these sets, but extension pieces and coupling-sets are also available.

To the right is a garden light set of German origin, which has been on the market for quite a long time. The light shines from round TL tubes, but the whole effect is rather cool and business-like, for the garden. A somewhat redder light is preferable.

The fitting in the somewhat over-exposed photograph immediately *below* is very well-known, and can be supplied for vertical and horizontal mounting. In the *centre* is an invention of an architect who did not want the lamps to be visible during the daytime. He concealed them by means of a tiny door behind the timbers of the house-front. There is no need for these fittings to be watertight, and the lamps themselves are not rainproof, though the box is.

If you want a plug contact in the garden, then the solution in the photo *centre below* is ideal. This too is a German design, as is the simple pillar-lamp *right*, which is lit by 3 bulbs. Exciting though lighting the garden is, it should always be remembered that electricity and water do not mix: if in doubt, consult an electrician.

Right two photographs of contemporary garden lamps, placed in good positions. *Below* The result that can be achieved with only a few lamps: the garden becomes an extension of the living-room in the evenings.

Soil-testing

The plants in your garden grow best when the nutrients are present in the ground in certain proportions. If there is something wrong with the way your plants grow, or if plant diseases are causing you a lot of trouble, it is wise to make a soil-test, or have one made. The most accurate result will be obtained by commissioning a professional laboratory for soil research to do this work. Most local authorities will do this for you. Some will do this free, but others make a small charge for doing it.

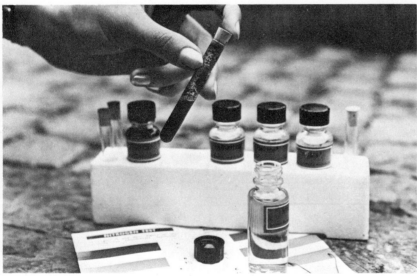

You can also carry out a soil-test yourself. You buy a soil-testing kit with which you can measure the percentage of nitrogen, phosphorus, potassium and the acidity (pH) of your soil. All you have to do is mix some soil with a reagent and shake the test-tube until the colour of the contents becomes stable. You then match the colour with the colour on a chart provided, and read off the pH value or whatever you are measuring. In some kits litmus paper is used, but the principle is the same.

Unless you are happy to waste money on plants that will certainly die in your soil, it is most important to find out whether it is acid or not. No rhododendrons, azaleas, camellias or heathers will grow unless it is acid.

Good digging is not so much a matter of back-breaking hard slog, as of working out what it is you are doing, and then taking it steadily. This can save one a great deal of extra work. On this page you see photographs of deep digging, or *digging two spits deep*. A 'spit' is the depth to which a spade penetrates the ground. The illustrations show an old lawn which needs to be deeply dug because the subsoil has become so compacted and impermeable that even the water will no longer soak away through it. The aim of the deep digging is, among other things, to create a crumbly soil structure. The idea is that the turves at the top finish up at the bottom at the end of the job.

The first job is to remove a row of turves (*below left*). Next a trench two spits deep is dug. The earth that is taken out of it is put to one side. At the end of the operation this soil will be put back again in the last remaining furrow. Standing in the two-spit deep furrow, the real work now begins (page 130, *above*). First the turf is stripped off (page 130, *below centre*) and laid upside down at the bottom of the trench. Then a

spadeful at a time the earth is cut up and turned over (page 130, *below right*). The diagram shows you more clearly what goes on. *Left* shows the system whereby lower and upper spit are interchanged. This system is only usable where there is no sharp distinction between top-soil and subsoil. In this case the turf is placed at the bottom of the trench, then the top spit goes on top of the turf, and after that the lower spit is laid upon that. By this time a new furrow has been created, and the process is repeated.

If the top-soil and subsoil are very different in character, then it is better to adopt the method shown in the diagram on the *right*. For this, a $1\frac{1}{2}$-spit furrow is dug out. The procedure is then to strip off the turf and lay it at the bottom of the first furrow. Then put the bottom spit of the second furrow on top of this. Finally the top spit of the third furrow is put on top of that, and the sequence followed again.

The photos on this page show two useful digging aids. *Left* is a spade of medium size made of stainless steel. The advantage of this material is its great strength, light weight, and above all the fact that the steel is always smooth and clean. Its only disadvantage is its high price. With a rusty spade one cannot work properly (soil clings to it).

The broad-tined digging fork (*below right*) is particularly suitable for working on clay soil (it clings less). It is also very handy for planting work.

Soil improvement

If you are content to grow in your garden only those plants which will grow there happily anyway, then you will have a rather dull garden. Most garden-owners want something more than this and to achieve this you need to create a *good loam*. But just what is a good loam?

A good loam is a soil that has a spongy, crumb-like structure. Because of this such soils are always open, and air can always reach to the roots of the plants. Moreover, such soil is never too wet or

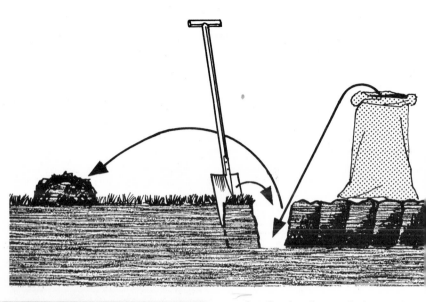

too dry. One hardly ever finds a garden where such soil occurs naturally. One therefore has to improve whatever soil one has got.

Clay soils are usually pretty well impermeable. Mixing in peat and sharp sand will improve them. Sandy soils are usually rather dry and infertile. Deep digging (page 130), adding a layer of organic manure to the base of the trench brings life to such soils. Subsoils and old builder's rubble and like, which are often left instead of top-soil by builders, are pretty infertile. By far the best plan is to remove such worthless soils, and replace them completely with good earth. If this cannot be done, then the only answer is just to keep on digging in peat, compost and manure until you have formed a good top-soil – a process which could take two or three years.

On the *opposite* page is a diagram explaining the process shown in photographs on this page. Here a small piece of ground is going to be used to grow rockplants. But it is too wet, so the first thing to do is to lay down a drainage layer of coarse grit or pebbles. For growing ordinary border plants a moisture-retaining material such as peat

or compost would be more suitable. First, at one side of the piece of ground to be improved, a channel is dug to the depth of one spit (*above left*). The excavated ground is carried to the other end of the plot, in this case simply on the spade (*above left*) – on bigger plots with the aid of a wheelbarrow. The furrow is not roughly dug out, but cut out neat and straight and brought to the required depth (*below left* and page 132).

The drainage material, in this case foam-plastic grains, is sprinkled into the furrow to the desired thickness (generally not more than 2–5 cm) (*below centre*). Then the second furrow is taken out, the earth being used to fill up the first furrow (*below right*). After carefully making the second furrow straight and clean, the drainage material is sprinkled in (page 134, *above left*) and the process is repeated. The last furrow is filled with the earth that came from the first. Digging may seem hard work, but once you have done it you will not need to do it again for some time.

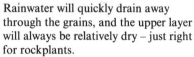

Rainwater will quickly drain away through the grains, and the upper layer will always be relatively dry – just right for rockplants.

A layered structure of this kind is not always desirable. Often one would rather have the drainage material

homogeneously distributed throughout a soil. This is most easily done with a rotavator, which for example is very suitable for mixing peat into a clay ground, or for enriching sandy soil with hop manure. In the case of smaller patches of ground, the work is better

done by hand, as when spreading stable manure over a dug plot (*above centre*). By shaking the fork the manure is made to fall in small fragments on the earth. Afterwards it is lightly dug in (*above right*).

	DIGGING	ADDITION	FERTILIZER
SANDY SOIL	2 spits deep, if tight-packed, loosen deeper.	Peat-soil, garden peat or peat dust or compost, to choice.	3–5 m³ rough stable manure. 5–20 kg lime, not simultaneously.
CLAY SOIL	1 spit deep, before the winter, so that the top layer gets well broken up by frost.	Peat dust, or perlite, to make the clay lighter.	1–3 m³ horse manure, or cow manure if the clay is poor in nutrients.
PEAT SOIL	1 spit.	Coarse grit.	1–3 m³ stable manure. 5–20 kg lime, not simultaneously.
SANDY-CLAY SOIL	1 to 2 spits.	If not light: peat.	1–3 m³ stable manure, lime mostly not necessary.
HEAVY or BLUE CLAY	In smaller gardens, if possible remove completely to a depth of 80 cm.	Replace by good peaty soil.	3–5 m³ rough stable manure. 5–20 kg lime, not simultaneously.

Drainage

In very low-lying ground when the water table may be rather high, drainage may be necessary to lower the water-level. Many shrubs cannot grow on too wet a subsoil. Their roots will not go deeper than the water table, and if this is very high, they will simply blow over. Many perennials, too, do very badly where there is a high water table.

The usual type of drainage, such as is often also applied to farmland, is illustrated in the large diagram. The drainpipes are bedded in rubble (or faggots) and empty directly into a ditch.

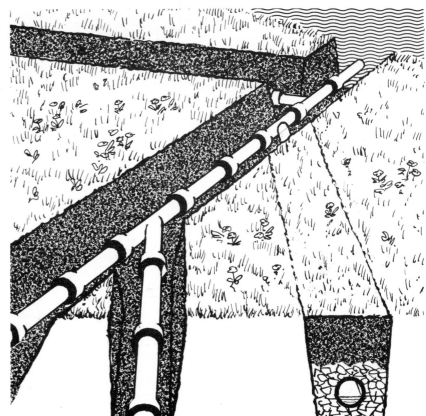

With this system one can only bring about a relatively small lowering of the water table. It does, however, enable the water to flow away more rapidly.

For laying a series of drains a narrow gully is sufficient, and a special spade (*photo*) is used.

The diagram (*bottom*) shows how the water gets into the drains.

If the water table needs to be lowered still more, then underground drainage helps (diagram *below right*). The drains empty into a well, from which the water can periodically be pumped into a ditch or foul-water drain.

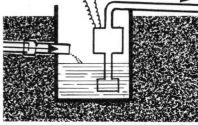

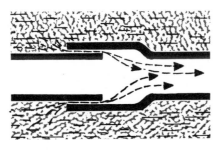

135

Compost

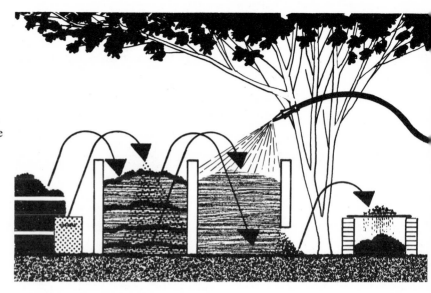

Making one's own compost is not only an ideal way of getting rid of garden and kitchen refuse: it also provides one of the finest of all possible soil foods. The compost is best prepared in special containers, of which two are needed. A loose pile soon becomes a rubbish-heap, and is a waste of space – untidy into the bargain. Examples of suitable containers are to be seen on this page. *Left* is the familiar plasticized iron grid type. *Centre* are two large concrete containers which harmonize well with many modern garden layouts. *Right* is an English plastic container, which retains moisture very well.

The general procedure is best shown by a diagram. The container on the left is used the first year. You throw all your grass mowings, weeds, kitchen refuse, etc. Do NOT include any stones, branches, plastic or glass.

When the layer is 15–20 cm thick, sprinkle on a little nitro-lime and a thin layer of peat (the sack and bale are on the extreme left).

When the container is full, after a year at the most, the half-done compost is lifted with a fork into the second container. Again, sprinkle in a little nitro-lime now and then. At the end of the second year the compost is sieved (*far right*) and is ready for use. The compost in-the-making should never be allowed to dry out. Hence the tree, which gives shade, and the garden hose.

Home-made compost unfortunately does not become hot enough to kill all the weed-seeds. It is, however, possible to sterilize the prepared compost chemically or with heat. Then you have a perfect mulch (see also page 43), which both feeds and improves the soil.

Planting shrubs

Every year millions of shrubs are planted. Of these about one in every ten dies – which is all very well for the nurseryman who can supply a new one, but is bitterly disappointing if it is your shrub that dies. The series of photos show you step by step precisely how shrubs should be planted.

If the shrubs are ordered from a dispatching-nursery, they generally arrive by carrier, packed in straw and plastic (*above right*). Providing they are kept out of frost, they can easily be left in this packing until the weekend. Once the planting-day arrives, they should be unpacked and sorted. Shrubs with balls of soil round the roots should be stood in a bucket of water to take in more moisture, the other sorts are laid out with a little straw on the roots to prevent drying (*above left*). Throw a few buckets of water over them.

The next step is to dig a big planting-hole

(*below left*). The bigger the hole the better. It should be about 60–80 cm deep, with straight sides and a flat bottom. When it is ready, tip in a barrow-load of good earth (*below centre*). Place the shrub on this, and, while it is firmly held in position, tip more earth around it (*below right*).

The next step is to water the shrub in when the hole is half-filled. This washes the soil well down among the roots (*above left*). All too often people forget to give this watering, and many shrubs die because they did forget it. When the

roots have been given a thorough soaking, the hole can be filled up further, the earth being firmly trodden down layer by layer. While this is going on the shrub must be held in place, for the position of the shrub can be altered by this treading.

Any strong stake can be used, but it must be sledge-hammered really firmly into the subsoil. The stake is placed in the hole at the same time as the tree, and in such a position that it is on the windward side (the west, in our case) (*below left*).

When finally the hole has been filled, make a little hollow round the stem, into which water can be poured. Repeat this watering in dry weather throughout the shrubs first summer.
Larger trees and bushes need a stake to keep them firmly upright. This is particularly important when they are first planted because of the developing, tender rootlets break off easily if the stem is moved to and fro by the wind.

When the stake is firmly in position, planting proceeds exactly as for shrubs. The roots are spread out so that the stake does not get in the way. The stem must not be allowed to chafe against the stake.

If a tree is to be planted in a paved garden, it is still necessary to make a large planting-hole (*below right*) however inconvenient this may be. If the soil is very poor, the hole may be filled with a mixture of the dug-out earth (70%) and peat or compost.

There are tree-ties and tree-ties. Each
has its different use. For smaller trees
plastic ties are best, like the one with the
buckle that you see *above left*. A little
block neatly maintains the distance
between tree and stake and prevents
rubbing. *Above centre* is a smaller type,
specially designed for standard roses.
Above right is a double plastic tie: the
broad part goes round the stake and the
narrow part round the tree. Don't forget
to loosen these ties little by little as the
tree grows thicker.

For heavier trees the canvas ties are
ideal (*centre left*). *Right* is a metal tie
with foam covering, specially designed
for trees with sensitive bark. *Below left* is
a black plastic perforated tie, suitable for
tying trees or bushes with many stems.
Right, a similar strip of heavier design,
suitable for tying normal trees.

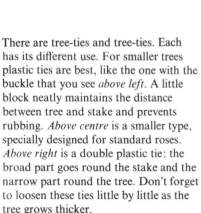

Protection

The most beautiful garden shrubs are all too often the most tender. One hard frost and you've lost them. Many beautiful border-plants are also sensitive, not only to frost, but also to an excess moisture in winter.

So long as the shrubs or plants are not too big, you can easily protect them. *Right* you see a Yucca, or Palm Lily, being wrapped up. The method is to use some white corrugated plastic (which reflects the sun, so doesn't over-heat), held upright by a few canes. The bottom of the plastic is pushed into the soil a little way. The space between plant and plastic is filled with reeds and straw. The plant can breathe, while it is at the same time protected from drying wind

and severe frost.

Below left. The protection of shrubs in tubs and containers is a problem that presents itself on balconies and patios. Push all the containers close together and set them up on boards (to protect them against cold feet). Pull a reed-mat round them and scatter straw or loose reeds over the plant. As soon as the

frost is over roll back the reed-mat otherwise the plants may start into growth too early in the season.

It is important to see that tender plants are covered up early enough in the year to protect them, usually towards the end of November. Protection should be kept on until the end of March or early April.

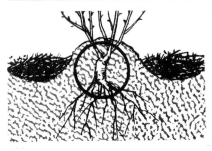

The protection of roses. Though roses are generally regarded as hardy, many varieties will suffer frost damage in the north of the country – and in a really severe winter could be killed by frost anywhere in the country.

The frost-sensitive point is the place of grafting which, it is true, is buried 5 cm under the earth on planting, but nevertheless is at risk. Roses should be earthed up in the autumn to protect this point. The soil between the bushes is carefully dug up and piled over the graft union (*below left*). The hollows between the roses are filled with stable manure. This provides an extra protection (see diagram).

With standard roses the task is somewhat more difficult. Here the graft is high above the ground, unprotected from frost. It is generally sufficient to tie the crown-branches together and cover them with a black, perforated plastic bag. This is fastened at the bottom with string. The plastic is not proof against heavy frost, but it does prevent the drying up of the wood.

Perennials protect themselves, at least when you let the dead foliage lie over the crowns through winter. In the spring this dead foliage is carefully cut from among the young shoots. Unfortunately the dead leaves are often cleared away to make 'the garden tidy for winter'! This is a bad practice. It exposes the young buds to the full severity of any heavy frost.

Weeds

By weeds we mean all those plants we don't want in the garden but which somehow manage to be there. They need to be kept down otherwise they will compete with and ultimately smother the plants we do want. Therefore, in one way or another, we need to get rid of them. The more bare soil there is visible in your garden, the more weeds you will get. Ground-cover plants (see page 27) are the best way of combating weeds. However, there will still be areas where weeds can grow. After a lot of weeding you may manage to get the top layer of soil weed-free. Once you start digging, the dormant seeds from the lower layer are brought up to the top (*diagram*) and you are back where you started.

Weeds that grow on paths and terraces between the stones can simply be treated chemically. The single-spray weedkillers with a basis of paraquat and

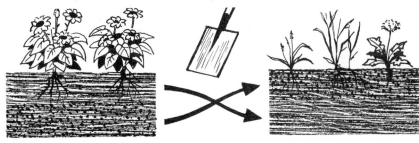

disquat are ideal elsewhere. They kill the green foliage of plants, but are neutralized as soon as they touch the soil. You can sow plant seeds again the next day. But beware! These weedkillers are VERY poisonous. By mounting a special sprinkler on a watering-can this type of weedkiller can also be used in planted areas so long as good care is taken that the foliage of plants that are wanted are not sprayed (page 143). Weeds in borders and clumps must always be pulled out by hand.

A new development is the chemical halting of the germination of weed-seeds. Firstly weed growth is removed and then the granules are sprinkled (*above*) or the fluid squirted on the soil. This will inhibit the germination of all seeds for the next six weeks or so.

Between groups of shrubs and other widely placed plants, weeds can be tackled by hoeing. Hoeing chops the tops of the weeds off their roots, and is best done in sunny weather, so that the cut weeds dry up. The best hoe for this job has a wave-edge and attachment on both sides of the blade (*below left*). When you buy a hoe, make sure that when you hold it in a normal standing

position the blade lies parallel with the ground (see the photos in the centre). The splendid stainless steel hoe (*left*) is not at the right angle. The photo *underneath it* shows the good position. Immediately *below* is a handy little stainless tool for handweeding, which gets the plants out of the ground root and all. For another method of fighting weeds, see mulching, page 43.

Ornaments

Garden ornaments conjure up unpleasant associations, as one promptly thinks of garden gnomes, rustic benches and other kitsch products. A garden ornament is only good when it adds to the atmosphere and character of the garden. The examples shown here are deliberately unusual examples, mainly made by sculptors; such ornaments are, of course, fairly expensive but on the other hand they do possess artistic value and are a fairly permanent asset like a painting. One can therefore look on the purchase of such an *objet d'art* as an investment rather than an expense. *Above* is the very restrained garden of a sculptor, that you have also seen elsewhere in this book in colour (page 24). The sculpture stands out very well against the rough concrete wall. The Southern Beech (*Nothofagus antarctica*) harmonizes particularly well. In the foreground is a Japanese azalea. The crowned peacock *right* is a contemporary work, specially produced for garden use. Such little sculptures do not have to be exorbitantly expensive.

Of old the sundial occupied an important place in the garden. It was useful for telling the time. In the modern garden, it can fulfil a usually decorative function, but the form of the sundial should be one that agrees with the architecture of house and garden. The sundial right is mass-produced in Spain, but the unusual form of the pointer and dial make it acceptable. *Far right* is a modern work of art in bronze, standing in Syon Park, London: rather costly but unique. Less expensive are relief plaques like the one *below*, which is the sort of thing you can make for yourself. It would then also be unique. Fibreglass or concrete are suitable materials to work in. *Bottom right* a statue made of pre-shaped concrete units, probably more suited to public parks than private gardens. Perhaps you see other possibilities for your own garden. The blocks can be glued with a resin putty or mortared.

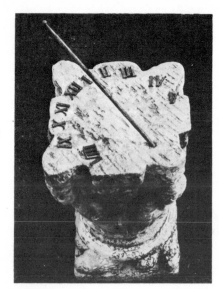

Birdbath

Birds are the most beautiful of living, voluntary garden ornaments. You entice them by feeding them, and also by offering them water. Many birds take a bath every day, for which water with a depth of 2–5 cm is needed. You can buy concrete vessels for this purpose, or you can also make a birdbath yourself. This is best done with reinforced concrete. Round or flat stones are pressed in the still-moist cement (*bottom right*).
The best birdbaths are those that have a water-connection, so that the water level can be best topped up without having to tote buckets. You can also install a small pump somewhere, so that the water can be kept circulating (*below left*). To clean out the bath a weekly rinsing-out with a powerful jet of water is all that is needed.

Levels

Most gardens are monotonously flat and it greatly enhances the garden if changes in level can be created. These make the garden seem larger, and create delightful little corners into which particularly interesting plants can be put, as well as opening up children's play. They also create more places for sitting down, and you have an added sense of protection.

In the old days it used to be fashionable to make changes in levels with lumps of rock – an imitation of alpine landscape. Nowadays it makes more sense to create differences of level where you can do something with them, as in the case of the sunken lounge, for example.

Differences of level need not be great; it would be somewhat overdoing it, for example, to construct metre-deep recesses in a small back-garden. Often a step down of 10–15 cm is sufficient. A good depth for a sunken lounge is 40–90 cm.

The simplest method of creating differences of level is with the aid of old railway sleepers. Because these do not require foundations it is possible to lay everything out to see the effect you are going to achieve before finally setting it in the ground. The large photo *above* shows a long-drawn-out stair of sleepers, the space between the sleepers being laid down to grass. This is not as impractical as it appears, for in practice you only walk on the sleepers. *Below left* on page 148 is a steeper stairway of sleepers. There is a fixed formula for stairs, which you should adopt if you want the steps to be comfortable to ascend. The riser should not be more than 9 inches high and the tread not less than 18 inches deep. The tread is the horizontal part of the stair, the riser is the vertical.

Levels can be constructed with other materials apart from sleepers. *Above right* is a U-shaped concrete element, outer measurements about $45 \times 45 \times 45$ cm. It is suitable for use as a retaining wall (left part of photo) but also very serviceable as steps. Because a step of 45 cm is too high, a row of these units is buried to half its height. You can see this construction very clearly on page 62.

A very charming effect can be created when the edges of the steps are not plainly visible, but masked by some overgrowing plants. This takes away much of the harshness of the layout, yet the clean, simple line remains. A good example is seen in the *lower* photo on the previous page. The steep stairway *below right* also gives a clear idea of this method. An excessive display of concrete is one of the greatest faults that modern garden architecture has to overcome. *Below left* a simple stair of wood paving-blocks. This material is pleasant to walk on, even with bare feet. The wood may need treating periodically with an algicide or fungicide to prevent it becoming slippery.

The patio in the photo *right* is a rather different affair. The brick sections are slightly cambered to allow rainwater to drain off through the gaps between the sections. A layer of rammed rubble serves as foundation.

Furniture

It is very difficult to be dogmatic about garden furniture since so much depends on personal taste. Nonetheless, having created an attractive garden it is important to have somewhere to sit and enjoy it, so a few ideas may not come amiss.

The chairs to the *right* are of plastic; the frame is of PVC-covered steel. The material lasts a long time and the chairs are very comfortable to sit on. The chairs *below* are of white-lacquered steel and there are various models. You can't sit on them for very long, but they are certainly decorative and can remain outside – as can the plastic chairs, for that matter.

The concrete benches shown *top right* are absolutely weatherproof and need no maintenance. Concrete is comfortable enough to sit on for half an hour, and you can always set out a few cushions. The group *below* has a somewhat rustic air, but it is not impractical and certainly not unsociable.

Below right are two good examples of modern slatted benches. The steel is sunk or concealed, and the seat is of tropical hardwood. You can make such benches yourself or have them made to your requirements.

If you like modern forms, then seats of polyester are ideal. They are not always comfortable for sitting on, but that is easily remedied with a few cushions. On the other hand, the material is decorative and imperishable. It can stay outside all the time.

Left is a concrete unit, here in use as a seat. Positioned differently the same unit can serve as a retaining wall or as a step. See also page 149. Height 45 cm.

The chair *below left* is very popular because it is easy to make yourself.

Right is a good idea for making a bench.

154

Afterword: by way of an introduction

In the photographs in this book you will often have seen the same gardens and the same models, illustrating all kinds of useful garden work. In the photograph *alongside* you see most of the people who have helped in making the gardens in this book.

Jan Haver is standing right at the back, in keeping with his modest nature. His contribution however was important: as a gardener of ten years' experience he is a much-photographed model, who also knows how tools should be handled. Beside him stands *Marijke Wierda*, who was the model for work on the lawn, among other things. *Wolfram Stehling* is seen on the extreme left. He is one of the world's best photographers of flowers and gardens. You will see his photographs throughout the book, especially on the colour pages. Beside him sits my wife *Iet*, who not only had all the fun of typing this manuscript but also had to cope with a lot of fuss and disorder and dozens of coffee-drinkers and eaters. I still don't understand why she never grumbled. On the extreme right in the centre is *Mr. A. F. M. Bruggen* of Elsevier Nederland N.V., with whom the first plans of this book were discussed. The content and execution are the result of our thorough deliberations. Beside him, in the black jacket, stands *Jaap Frank*, who designed the book. In the foreground sits *Betty Hogervorst*, whom you will recognize from many of the photos. Every day for months she has been busy with the book, not only as regards posing, but also in connection with drawings, darkroom work and layout. In short, a girl of many talents. Of myself, I will only say that I have worked on this book with much pleasure. I am very grateful to all my co-workers and to the publisher who have all done so much to make this book all that I hoped it would be.

ROB HERWIG

Index